CAPILANO COLLEGE

P9-EEK-068

WITHDRAWN

M 03/96 695

Why Poverty Persists in India

A Framework for Understanding the Indian Economy

To
Viju
and
Truus, Tai and Sadanand

Why Poverty Persists in India

A Framework for Understanding the Indian Economy

MUKESH ESWARAN and ASHOK KOTWAL

DELHI

OXFORD UNIVERSITY PRESS

BOMBAY   CALCUTTA   MADRAS

1994

60108476

Oxford University Press, Walton Street, Oxford OX2 6DP

Oxford   New York   Toronto
Delhi Bombay Calcutta Madras Karachi
Kuala Lumpur Singapore Hong Kong Tokyo
Nairobi Dar es Salaam Cape Town
Melbourne Auckland Madrid

and associates in

Berlin Ibadan

© *Oxford University Press 1994*
ISBN   0 19 563238 9

This book is published in association with
THE BOOK REVIEW LITERARY TRUST, NEW DELHI

Typeset by Urvashi Press, Meerut 250 001
Printed at Rajkamal Electric Press, Delhi 110 033
and published by Neil O'Brien, Oxford University Press
YMCA Library Building, Jai Singh Road, New Delhi 110 001

Contents

Acknowledgements

We would like to thank our many friends and well-wishers who have read this manuscript, made helpful suggestions, and given us encouragement. These include Brian Copeland, David Donaldson, Vinayak Eswaran, Patrick Kenny, P. Khadekar, Barry Morrison, Keizo Nagatani, Avinash Paranjape, Setty Pendakur, John Roemer, Anand Swamy, Prashant Vankudre, and John Wood. We are especially indebted to Kumar Eswaran, Anji Redish, and Dan Usher for detailed comments on an earlier draft. We would also like to thank Nancy Lyon for her patience and for her efficient word processing of the manuscript, and Pierre Brochu for some research assistance.

1

Introduction

It is not only economists who are interested in economics. The economic performance of a country affects all its people, and most people have some curiosity about it. This is especially true of people in less developed countries (LDCs). The process of development transforms a society in fundamental ways. People who have toiled in the fields for generations leave their land and trek to the cities looking for work in industries. Labour tasks get specialized in every conceivable way. Markets develop connecting distant parts of the economy and creating a complex system which seems to have a logic of its own. This logic seems quite incomprehensible to a layperson. Some groups in the society gain and others lose as the economy develops. Inevitably, there is social turmoil. Almost every government policy is beset by controversy. Even the so-called experts seem to differ widely in their opinions on economic policies. Consider the wide spectrum of opinions heard on the new direction of economic policy announced by the Rao government in 1991:

Unrestricted capitalism will serve interests of only the rich. —Stagnation in India is caused by excessive government control of the economy and there is an urgent need for liberalization. —Trade with developed countries will only benefit the rich by giving them easy access to Western-style consumption goods and, in fact, will hurt the poor by causing de-industrialization of the Indian economy. —Trade has been an engine of growth in the successful transformation of many Asian economies like South Korea, Taiwan, Malaysia and Indonesia, and so will it be for India.

There is a bewildering array of opinions. Sometimes the differences stem from the different criteria used for measuring the performance of an economic system which, in turn, may be based on differences in ethical priorities. Sometimes they result from differences in perceptions of how an economic system works. One yearns for some clarification of these issues. But economists usually are of no help. They talk to each other in a language that nobody else can understand. Physicists do the same and so do chemists and biologists, but people do not feel quite so deprived. It seems perfectly acceptable to go through life without understanding the process of fusion or the molecular structure of a polymer. It is bothersome, however, to have to take the word of some expert on whether we are on the right course of economic development. It may be helpful to have a simple conceptual framework that one can use to assess the myriad of opinions on the course of Indian development that crowd newspapers and energize political campaigns.

Our goal in this book is to present such a conceptual framework and use it to lay bare the logic asssociated with the process of economic development. Although our framework is general enough to be applied to any labour-abundant poor country, we have used it specifically to analyse the course of India's development since independence. The orientation of this book is theoretical rather than empirical. We do not dwell on any specific policy measures such as the recent moves to liberalize or the various rural development schemes. Nor do we deal with any short-term problems such as government deficits or depleting foreign exchange reserves. Instead, we concentrate on building a convenient framework for thinking about some broad and long-term processes at work in a developing economy. We believe that this framework can be used to analyse the policy implications for the general health of the economy. It is not designed, however, to facilitate thinking about temporary illnesses such as indebtedness to other countries which result from poor health of the economy. What distinguishes this book from other such theoretical exercises in the field of Development Economics is that we have addressed it to a reader who has had no formal training in economics. We have used no mathematics, and have tried to keep jargon to an absolute minimum. Wherever we have found it convenient to use a special terminology we have made an effort to first explain it in simple English. All the essential economic concepts are introduced from scratch. Despite this, the book probably does not make light reading.

In this chapter, we take a cursory look at how far India has progressed since independence, identify some important stylized facts, and introduce the reader to the approach used in this book.

Progress Since Independence

Under British rule, the Indian economy stagnated for over a hundred years prior to independence. The national income grew only at around 1 per cent per annum. But because of high mortality rates the population also grew at a slow rate (round 1 per cent), preventing a decline in the per capita income. In 1947, at the time of independence, India was primarily an agrarian economy and its industrial sector accounted for less than 15 per cent of national income and employed less than 10 per cent of the labour force. The textiles sector had a lion's share of both of these. Apart from steel and some light engineering goods, Indian industry produced only a small range of manufactured goods. The technological capabilities of India were definitely very limited at the time of independence.

After independence, the government actively promoted industrialization. As a result, India today is a major industrial and military power. It produces a wide range of different industrial goods including such sophisticated products as computers, military aircrafts, automobiles, and locomotives. It has launched its own weather satellites into space. Its universities have produced one of the largest pools of scientists and engineers in the world.

— Independence certainly broke the spell of stagnation in the Indian economy. The national income showed a trend growth rate of 3.6 per cent per annum over the period of 1950–84. Improvements in public health measures brought down mortality rates. This proved to be a mixed blessing, as it caused the rate of population growth to nearly double, whittling down the gains in per capita income to only 1.5 per cent per annum. These income gains would not have been possible without a substantial contribution from the industrial sector. The trend growth rate of the industrial sector was 5.0 per cent per annum during the same period, while that of agriculture was only 2.2 per cent which was almost the same as the rate of population growth over this period. Consequently, the contribution of the industrial sector to the national income had increased from 15 per cent in 1947 to 26 per cent in 1988. A notable feature of this industrial growth is that it has not resulted in a significant increase in the percentage of total labour employed by industry; the change has been from 10 per cent to 15 per cent in 40 years. Consequently, the percentage of India's labour force employed in agriculture and its allied activities has changed only from 74 to 66 in the same period.

The growth performance of the Indian economy, though an improvement over the pre-independence period, has been quite lacklustre. India remains one of the poorest countries in the world. Its per capita income is about 6% of the per capita income of the United States—a country whose lifestyle India's elite try to mimic. Fig. 1.1 compares the growth performance of India with those of some other developing countries from Asia over the period 1950–80. The per capita income of each country is indicated in the figure as the percentage of the per capita income in the United States. The comparison with South Korea is especially startling. In 1950, both South Korea and India had almost the same per capita income at about 7% of that of the United States, and in 1980 this percentage had improved to 25 per cent for South Korea while it had remained virtually unchanged for India. Fig. 1.1 also indicates that countries like Malaysia and Thailand have shown a superior performance to India's. It is clear from this figure that these Asian countries, unlike India, have grown at faster rates than the United States.

Not only is India a very poor country, but its income is unequally distributed, as in many other countries in the Third World. The top 20 per cent of the population in India have a share of more than 40 per cent of the total consumption expenditure (i.e. income minus saving) while the share of the bottom 40 per cent is less than 20 per cent. The distribution of income is even more skewed than that of consumption expenditure. As a result, the poorest in India (typically, landless agricultural workers) are exceedingly poor. Even by the most conservative estimate, over 35 per cent of Indians were below the official poverty line in 1987. (The Sixth Five Year Plan defined an all-India poverty line as a per capita consumption expenditure of Rs 65 at 1977–8 prices in rural areas corresponding to a calorie intake of 2,400, and Rs 75 in urban areas corresponding to a calorie intake of 2,100.) According to the World Bank data for 1985, the poverty statistics were worse for India than for sub-Saharan Africa.

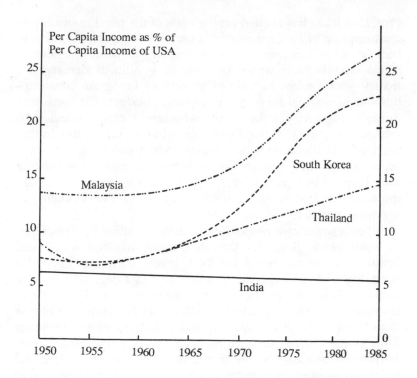

Source: *Income and Wealth*, Series 34, March 1988.

FIG. 1.1   *Relative Growth Performance of India*

What is even more alarming is the fact that the percentage of population below the poverty line is higher and yet falling more slowly in India than in other less developed Asian countries like Indonesia, Malaysia, and Thailand. It is likely that the distribution of income has worsened in India over the last forty years.[1]

[1]Although the consumption expenditure data gathered by National Sample Survey do not indicate such a trend in the distribution of consumption expenditure, it has been argued by Prof. Sundrum of Australian National University that there is under reporting of expenditure on non-food grain items and that suitably adjusted data would, in fact, show a worsening trend in distribution.

Prof. Dandekar has argued on the basis of the trend in per capita consumption of foodgrains that a very small part of the gains in India's national income have been trickling down to the poor. A simple test is to compare the rate of growth of demand for luxury goods with the rate of growth of foodgrain consumption—the principal item in a poor man's budget. The consumer durable industry (i.e. two-wheelers, cars, televisions, refrigerators, etc.) is the fastest growing sector in the Indian economy. At the same time, despite widespread hunger, there is accumulation of grain stocks with the government indicating that the poor lack purchasing power. This suggests in a compelling way that the income gains from economic development are accruing mostly to the rich.

When a significant percentage of the population is so poor that its basic needs like adequate diet, clean drinking water, and health care are not being satisfied, health indicators like child mortality and life expectancy reflect this fact. Fig. 1.2 below illustrates how poorly India compares with other Third World countries. Once again, not only is the child mortality rate higher than it is in Indonesia, Malaysia, and Thailand, but it is declining more slowly than in any of these countries. On the literacy front, India's performance is one of the worst in the world. (Fig. 1.3 gives a cross-country comparison between India and some Asian countries.) In 1947, 19 per cent of India's population could read and write. By 1985, this statistic had improved to only 43 per cent. In the same time period, China has improved the literacy rate from 30 per cent to 70 per cent, and South Korea from 32 per cent to 95 per cent. India's performance is especially shocking in the light of its achievements in higher education.

The above statistical picture merely confirms what casual observation would reveal about the course of India's development. Increases in income, moderate as they are, have been confined mostly to the thin upper crust of the society. Consumer durables like two-wheelers, refrigerators, and video recorders are now becoming commonplace in upper-class households. Even an automobile is no longer beyond the reach of many salaried employees in the modern sector, whether public or private. No university professor in India could afford a car 45 years ago. Now, he or she can. No bank clerk could then imagine a family vacation at a holiday resort. Now, he or she can. The living

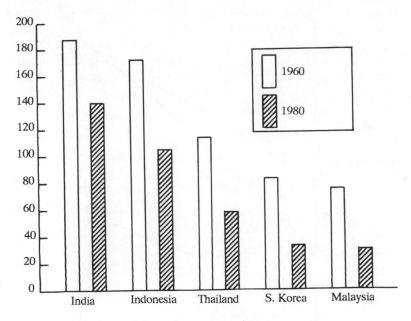

Source: *World Development Report 1982.* (The World Bank)

FIG 1.2 *Child Mortality—Cross-country Comparison in Asia.*
(deaths of children aged 0–4 years for every 1000 live births)

standards of a segment of the Indian population have certainly risen over the last 45 years. The 'demonstration effect', a term coined to capture the attempt by the elite in poor countries to mimic the Western lifestyle, is quite noticeable in India. This is what is fuelling the growth in luxury goods industries, the fastest growing sector within the manufacturing sector. Clearly, India has taken some significant strides in modernizing its economy and there have been tangible benefits for a part of its population.

But this is a world within a far different world. Even within a city like Bombay, the skyscrapers housing the air-conditioned corporate offices are located not too far from some of the worst slums in the world. Many of these slums lack basic amenities like running water and sanitation. They are infested with crime and disease, nipping in the bud any aspirations the children of the poor may have for a better life. Yet, no matter how dreadful life is

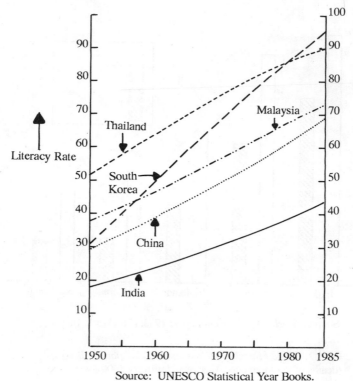

Source: UNESCO Statistical Year Books.

FIG. 1.3 *Literacy Rate in Asian Countries.*

(percentage of population above 15 years of age who can read and write)

in the city slums, it can only be better than in the rural areas from where thousands flee to the cities every day in search of a better life. The most oppressive fact of life in rural India is the scarcity of employment opportunities. Agriculture in many parts of India is still heavily dependent on rainfall, and when the rains fail even seasonal jobs like harvesting are in short supply. There is no evidence that landless labourers who occupy the bottom-most rung on the income ladder have become better off or diminished in numbers over the last forty years.

The course of economic development in India conjures up an image of a balloon rising, with a tiny part of India's population aboard, slowly toward Western standards of consumption,

leaving the rest at the subsistence level. Such lopsided development is likely to breed widespread resentment and sow the seeds
of destruction of the present political system. Even the elite who
have been gaining from economic growth so far have reasons to
worry about its present course. Why poverty persists in India
despite noticeable industrial progress and what should be done
about it, are not, therefore, merely academic questions.

A Sketch of the Analytical Framework

It might be helpful at this point to get at least vaguely acquainted
with the ideas that will form the main building blocks of our
framework. Our purpose in introducing them at this point is to
make sure that the discussion on the adopted approach that will
follow this sub-section will make sense to the reader.

Table 1.1
Richer countries have a lower percentage of labour in agriculture

Country	Per capita income	Percentage of labour in agriculture in 1980
Nepal	490	93
India	614	70
China	1619	74
Indonesia	1063	57
South Korea	2369	36
Malasia	3112	42
Ireland	4929	19
New Zealand	7363	11
Australia	8349	7
Japan	8117	11
Canada	11332	5
United States	11404	4

Note: Per capita income figures have been adjusted according to the purchasing
power of each country.

Source: Income and Wealth, Series 34, March 1988.

Table 1.1 reveals an interesting regularity about the process of
economic development. The richer the country, the smaller is the

percentage of the labour force engaged in agriculture. Even the largest grain-exporting countries of the world like the United States, Canada, and Australia, have less than 7% of their labour force employed in agriculture. A hundred years ago a substantial part of the labour force in each of these countries was engaged in agriculture. As these countries industrialized, labour shifted from agriculture to industry. Either the labour force remaining in agriculture produced enough food for the entire population (through increases in productivity) or some of the industrial production was exported to other countries in exchange for food. In a market economy, labour from agriculture can be enticed to move to another sector only by an offer of a higher wage. The labour remaining in agriculture would also experience an increase in their wages since each worker would now have a greater amount of land to work with, and would be, therefore, more productive (i.e. have higher output per worker). A continuous movement out of agriculture would thus be accompanied by a continuous increase in wages. Such a movement of labour between sectors would be possible because there is either a technological improvement in agricultural production (i.e. agricultural productivity growth) or an increase in industrial exports or both. Agricultural productivity growth and industrial exports are thus intimately connected with the disappearance of poverty from any economy. Both these measures impinge on poverty by increasing the supply of food domestically.

An implicit assumption here is that industrial goods do not substitute very well for food. If the economy is successful in generating an abundance of textiles, people are not likely to wear more clothes and eat less because clothes have now become relatively cheaper. Human beings are capable of making a choice, but they follow some biological imperatives. When people are close to subsistence, these biological imperatives matter much more than free choice. Only after one's hunger is appeased, would an individual be interested in spending one's money on other things. And even then there is likely to be an hierarchy of needs. After food, he may want to spend on some basic industrial goods like clothing, and only after that need is satisfied to a certain minimum extent would the individual think of luxuries like a television. A family's expenditure pattern depends very much on its income level. The poor spend most of their in-

DAMAGE NOTED

comes on food while the rich constitute almost exclusively the
market for the products of modern industry. When an economy
is underdeveloped and there is only a small part of the population rich enough to buy industrial goods, there is no incentive for
anyone to set up an industry unless he can tap the demand for
such goods in the already-developed part of the world. Table 1.2
indicates how households in poorer countries spend greater
shares of their incomes on food and very little on industrial
goods. Tanzania, the poorest country in the table, spends 62 per
cent on food and 18 per cent on the items in the last two columns
which account for all the industrial consumption other than
clothing and footwear (namely medical services, education, and
transportation, and other consumption including consumer
durables). In contrast, the United States, the richest country in
the sample, spends only 19 per cent on food and 63 per cent on
the latter items.

Table 1.2
Composition of total household consumption (1980–5)

Country	Per capita income in 1980 US $	Food	Clothing and footwear	Rent, fuel and Power	Healthcare, education, and transport	Other consumption
Tanzania	355	62	12	8	8	10
India	750	52	10	8	18	12
Indonesia	1255	48	7	13	10	22
Thailand	1900	34	11	6	25	24
S. Korea	3056	35	6	11	21	27
Malaysia	3415	30	5	9	29	27
Ireland	5205	22	5	11	28	28
New Zealand	8000	12	6	14	34	34
West Germany	10708	12	7	18	32	31
Canada	12196	11	6	21	31	32
US	12532	13	6	18	36	27

Source: *Income and Wealth*, Series 34, March 1988 and *World Development Report*,
        1988: The World Bank.

Our framework, thus, is based on simple ideas that are consistent with common-sense. The challenge is to weave them into a cohesive whole. There are two types of errors that a person untrained in economics is liable to make while thinking about economic issues. First, while assessing the costs and benefits of any action, he may ignore the costs and benefits of an alternative foregone as a result of that action. (These are referred to as *opportunity costs*.) For example, when an agricultural worker shifts to industry the agricultural output that he is no longer producing should be considered a cost to the economy. Or, when a government decides to increase the subsidy to farmers or to exporters, it is reducing expenditure on some other item in the economy and the effects of this should be considered in the analysis. Secondly, laymen underappreciate the inter-connectedness of a modern economy. For example, whether some enterepreneur in Bombay organizes an industry to produce garments for an export market may seem irrelevant to the well-being of an agricultural worker toiling in a village in Bihar, but it is not. As some labour is moved out of agriculture, there would be a tendency for the wage rate in agriculture to rise. One reason for building a model or a framework is to incorporate into our thinking these fundamental concepts of *opportunity costs* and *general equilibrium* (i.e. inter-connectedness).

Thinking about such a complex inter-connected system is difficult without the simplifying tool of a model. The primary function of the model presented in this book is to facilitate our thinking about this complex system. In a market economy, the producers produce what the consumers will buy and what consumers will want to buy depends upon their incomes, which in turn depend upon what is being produced. To avoid falling into the trap of circular reasoning, we need to adopt an approach that will abstract from unimportant details and clear the corridors through which logical analysis can proceed without hindrance.

The Approach

The approach we adopt in this book has many limitations. It makes complex social processes look very stark and abstract. The reader may feel uncomfortable in this imaginary world where people have only one dimension; they are trying to maximize their economic gains. They are stripped of all other motivations such as the ones stemming from their regional affinities, altruism, or malice. It cannot be denied that these factors play a big role in the way people behave, especially in India. But these factors are not central to the story we want to tell. We believe that the most important behavioural characteristic of human beings in the process of economic development is a search for personal economic gains. Thus we give self-interested behaviour the centre stage. The richness that characterizes a good social essay is the price we will pay to gain clarity.

In the quest to simplify, we will make highly unrealistic assumptions. For example, we assume that the poor spend all their money on food. Clearly, the poor have other needs like clothing, shelter, fuel and transportation. But the conclusions we draw are still valid when the poor spend very little (15 per cent of their incomes, for the bottom 20 per cent in India) on items other than food. By making a stark assumption we get sharp conclusions which give us insights into the way things work qualitatively. For example, this stark assumption about the way people spend their money will lead to a conclusion that, in the absence of trade, industrial progress will have no impact on the well-being of the poor at all. When the poor do spend some money on things other than food, textiles for instance, industrial progress will have some impact on their well-being. However, to the extent they spend very little money on these goods, this impact will be small. In other words, stark assumptions bring out in a forceful and clear way the causal links in a complex process. A model incorporates the essential behaviour of the key players whose interaction is the focus of attention. The simpler the model, the easier it is to make thought-experiments on the model and to generate predictions. The purpose of this book is to present such a model of the process of development of an agrarian economy and then use it to shed some light on the question of why poverty has persisted in India.

One surprise awaiting the reader is that we have depicted the Indian economy as a market economy. We also assume that the producers in India are guided in their choices of what to produce by the market demand, stemming from the way consumers choose to spend their money. This may seem a bit unrealistic in the Indian context since India has had central planning for the last forty years. The Indian economy, however, is basically a market economy, albeit one with a great deal of government intervention.[2] Producers' decisions are mainly guided by what (and how much) will sell in the market. Indian planners have always decided on investment allocations only after estimating the demand for various goods and services. Our analysis, as we have already seen, focuses on the interaction between agriculture and industry and on the movement of labour between them. We believe that this interaction is primarily driven by market forces and, therefore, we depict the Indian economy as if it were a market economy.

In this book, starting from first principles, we develop a framework which enables us to arrive at some conclusions regarding the process of development in India. We make an attempt to spell out clearly the logic that leads to these conclusions. Some of these, stated starkly, are as follows. In the absence of international trade, industrial progress may have only a minimal effect on the well-being of the poor. Technical progress in agriculture, on the other hand, invariably benefits the poor. Only when agriculture is sufficiently advanced do the benefits of industrial progress trickle down to the poor. Whether the poor in India gain or lose from international trade depends on how the rate of technical progress in India compares with that elsewhere. If the rate of technical progress is slower in India, the poor in India lose; if it is faster, they gain. Whether or not a boom in the agricultural exports of India benefits the poor depends on what causes the boom. If it is due to an increase in foreign demand, the poor in India become worse off. On the other hand, if the boom is due to rapid technical progress in Indian agriculture, the poor become better off.

In the next chapter, we present an introduction to some basic notions in economics. In the third chapter we will present the main model which captures the interconnectedness of a less developed economy, making it possible to analyse the movement of labour between agriculture and industry. We devote three

[2]Prof. Kaushik Basu asserted in a symposium organized by *India Today* that India should be regarded as more of a market economy than many countries commonly regarded as market economies. 'Where else could you buy a driver's licence?', he asked rhetorically.

chapters to an analysis of the effects of technical progress in various sectors. We will analyse in two chapters the implications for India of participating in trade with the developed world. One chapter is devoted to an examination of how India's industrial policy hampered technical progress in industry. In the last chapter we will try to tie all the different arguments presented in this book into one coherent theme.

2

Some Essential Concepts

In this chapter we introduce, at a broad level, the economic concepts that are essential to understanding this book. We presume that the reader has had no formal training in economics. So we attempt to motivate the need for the conceptual tools introduced here. After receiving an overview of the essential economic notions in this chapter, the reader will find that his or her understanding is enhanced by their repeated application in the rest of the book.

Economic development is concerned with how the well-being (or welfare) of people improves over time. There are, of course, innumerable factors that impinge on people's welfare: the consumption of various goods and services, their level of health, the amount of leisure they have available, freedom from political repression, freedom from religious persecution, freedom of speech, etc. In this book, we are concerned only with the *economic* welfare of people. So we focus exclusively on one measure of welfare: the amounts of various goods and services consumed. The greater the amounts consumed, the higher is the level of welfare. If the process of economic development enables a person to consume more of at least one good, without requiring him to curtail consumption of any of the others, then surely we can say that the person is getting better off, i.e. his welfare is improving.

In any economy there are literally thousands of goods consumed. Allowing for as many goods in our conceptualization would not only be tedious but counter-productive: it would needlessly clutter our thinking. So we restrict attention to two or three goods which are to be interpreted as representatives of broad classes of goods. These broad classes are not chosen arbitrarily; they are judiciously selected so as to identify those that play a pivotal role in the developmental process. Except in one chapter of this book, we consider only two such representative goods. These are Grain and Textiles. (We use these terms as proper nouns to remind us all along that each of them represents an entire class of goods.) Grain stands for all the goods that can be thought of as food. It is the output of the agricultural sector of an economy. So Grain is proxy for rice, wheat, corn, legumes, etc. Textiles stand for all the goods that can be thought of as necessary for good living but are not absolutely essential for survival (as food is). So Textiles are a proxy for clothing, housing, footwear, kitchenware, bicycles, etc. They are products of the industrial sector of an economy.

Now that we have reduced the number of goods produced by the economy to essentially two, we have to understand how an economy resolves two important questions, which determine the well-being of its people:

1. What are the factors that determine how much of these goods will be produced in the economy?
2. What determines how the goods produced will be allocated across the different people of the economy? In other words, how is it decided how much of these goods the workers get to consume, how much the landlords, how much the capitalists, and so on?

We shall first examine in this book the developmental process of a purely market-based economy. The essential characteristic of a free-market economy is that the amounts produced of various goods, their prices, and the distribution of incomes across the various members of the population are all determined by the forces of demand and supply. The government plays little or no role in deciding these questions. The reader need not be alarmed that the analysis to be presented in this book will be irrelevant to India because the government has played a major role in Indian development over the past four decades. It is only by clearly understanding what the market system can and cannot do that we can appreciate what the government might do to improve matters. It must be realized, however, that governments can also introduce inefficiencies and problems that might have been absent. We shall have a lot to say about this in later chapters.

We now turn to the consideration of the notions of demand and supply in a market economy.

The Demand Side

By the demand side of a market we mean a characterization of the things that determine how much of the goods in question are demanded by consumers. The most obvious determinants of a consumer's demands for goods are the consumer's income and the prices of the goods. The income sets a limit on how much the person can spend (in the absence of borrowing), and the prices determine how much of the goods the consumer can purchase or demand with his income. In other words, the prices of goods together with an individual's income determine his *purchasing power*. A consumer can only demand from the market goods in amounts that he can afford. In the sense in which the term is used, demands must be backed by purchasing power. A poor person may be very needy, but those needs may not be translated into demands for various goods in the markets because they do not have the incomes to pay for their needs. We shall return later to the question of how the incomes of economic agents and the prices of goods are determined. Suppose, for the moment, these are given.

How does a consumer decide how much of his income he should spend on one good as opposed to another? Given his income, how much Grain should he demand and how much Textiles? In other words, what determines the composition of his demands? The most important determinant of the composition of a consumer's demand is *tastes*. The term tastes (or preferences, as it is often called) unfortunately has a frivolous connotation to it. But there is nothing frivolous or whimsical about it. In general, tastes may be determined by a person's innate psychological make-up. For the categories of goods we consider here, tastes are dictated by the even more innate biological instinct for survival, and by the extent to which the goods serve this biological end.

In this book, the tastes we attribute to people are based on the idea that they have a list of strict priorities. Only after the most important priority has been dealt with, will consideration be given to the next priority, and so on. Since the most essential consideration is clearly the biological imperative of survival, food is the most important priority in a consumer's tastes. What this means is that a consumer will first spend his income on Grain, and only after he has had enough to eat (20 kilograms of Grain a month, for example) will he purchase or demand any Textiles. If he exhausts his income before he consumes 20 kilograms of Grain, he will demand no Textiles. On the other hand, if he has sufficient income, once he consumes 20 kilograms of Grain, the rest of his income he spends entirely on Textiles.

We shall refer to the tastes described above as *hierarchical tastes*. This is to reflect the fact that people, especially in a poor country, have a hierarchy of needs, which they meet in the order dictated. This characterization of tastes, because it is stark, simplifies our conceptual thinking about the developmental process. But more importantly, it is a fairly realistic representation of the tastes of people in a developing country. Empirical evidence clearly shows that people with very low incomes spend a very high proportion of their income on food. In India, the poorest 65% of the population spends 82% of its income on food. The proportion of income spent on food becomes smaller as the income gets higher and higher. We shall see in this book, that this simple and realistic premise upon which we model tastes has enormous consequences for the manner in which economic development impinges on the various classes of society.

Given these tastes, and the prices of Grain and Textiles, we can determine how much a consumer with a given income will demand of Grain and of Textiles. Typically, the higher the price of a good, the less of the good will be demanded. By adding up the demands of all the people in the economy, we can obtain the total demands for Grain and Textiles.

The Supply Side

In response to the demand for goods from consumers, in a market system a supply will arise from producers. In any given year, an economy is endowed with different amounts of various resources like labour, land, capital, etc. These resources can be used as inputs to produce as outputs the goods that are desired by society. Producers will use these inputs and the prevalent technology to produce and sell goods in the amounts desired, with the intention of making profits. In compensation for the services provided, producers will make the owners of these inputs a payment commensurate with the contribution of the inputs. These payments are, in fact, what constitute the incomes of various people in the economy. It is this that puts purchasing power in their hands to demand goods for consumption in the first place. How much will the various inputs be paid in a market system for their services in production? To answer this important question, we need to first introduce some concepts pertaining to the production process and acquire some understanding of the workings of the market system.

Production

In order to produce a good, producers will have to use some technology that is available to them. The technology of production will dictate which inputs are required for producing the good. For example, the agricultural technology would normally specify that the production of Grain requires land and labour. The technology also dictates in what combinations the inputs are required to produce various levels of output; more output requires more by way of inputs. If we want to double the output of Grain (from 500 kilograms, say) we can do so by using double the amount of land and double the amount of labour. Suppose it is unfeasible for a producer to increase the amount of land he cultivates. Will it be impossible for him to double the output? Not necessarily, since he can compensate for the fixity of the amount of land used by using more than twice the amount of labour. In other words, it is usually possible to produce a given output level (say, 1,000 kilograms of Grain) by using more than one combination of inputs. These combinations are such that if we use less of one input we have to compensate for it by using more of the other, so as to produce the same level of output.

Since the inputs can be used in different combinations, how is a producer to decide which is the most appropriate combination? His choice will depend on how productive, or useful, the inputs are in contributing to output. Consider an example. A farmer cultivates a one hectare farm with one worker's labour, and the total output (i.e. *total product*) is, say, 50 kilograms of Grain per month. Now suppose he holds fixed the amount of land and successively adds more and more labour by hiring workers, as a result of which the total product per month with 2 workers, 3 workers, 4 workers, and 5 workers is given, respectively, by 90 kilograms, 120 kilograms, 140 kilograms, and 150 kilograms of Grain, respectively. The contribution to output of an additional worker is referred to as the *marginal product* of labour. The marginal product of the very first worker is 50 kilograms, of the second 40 (= 90 – 50) kilograms, third 30 kilograms, fourth 20 kilograms, and of the fifth 10 kilograms.

Notice that in the above example, the addition of each worker increases the total product, but this increase is less than that of the previous worker. In other words, the marginal product of each worker decreases as we add more and more workers to a given plot of land, as illustrated by the curve AB in Fig. 2.1. Why is this? It is because as we keep adding workers, holding fixed the amount of land, each worker gets less and less land to work with and so his productivity declines. When there is only one worker, he gets to work with one hectare of land. When there are two workers, each gets only half a hectare of land, and so on. This is an example of a general principle known as the *law of diminishing returns*. It states that, in a production process, if one or more inputs are fixed, the marginal products of the other inputs will ultimately start declining. (In our example, the marginal product of labour starts declining from the very beginning.) This principle will prove very important for us and will be repeatedly invoked in our analysis. When we look at the agricultural sector of the economy as a whole, the total amount of land is fixed. Thus, there will be diminishing returns, i.e. declining marginal product, to adding more and more labour to this sector. It is important to grasp the point that diminishing returns to an input will obtain only if the amount used of one (or more) of the other inputs is fixed. If there are no inputs other than labour used in a production process, for example, the marginal product of labour would be constant, i.e. the marginal product of labour would not diminish as more and more labour is used.

Just like we defined the marginal product of labour, we can define the marginal product of land or of any other input. In the

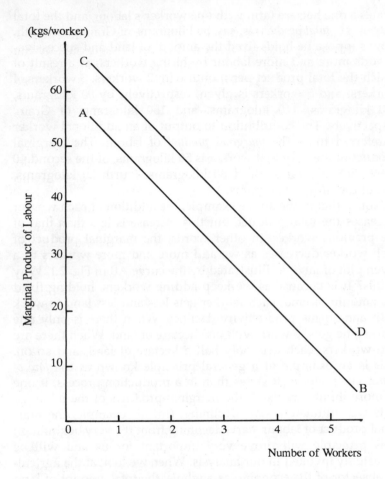

(kgs/worker)

Marginal Product of Labour

Number of Workers

FIG. 2.1 *Illustrates diminishing marginal returns to labour when
the amount of land used is held fixed.*

above example, the marginal product of land would be defined
as the increase in output brought about by an additional hectare
of land, when the amount of labour used is held fixed.

Let us now turn to the question of how much each additional
worker is worth to the farmer. Suppose the price of Grain is Rs 3
per kilogram. The very first worker's marginal product (i.e. contribution to output) is 50 kilograms of Grain, which is worth Rs

150. This is called the *value of the marginal product* of the first worker. It tells us how much the first worker is worth to the farmer, because that is the amount of revenue generated by the worker. Similarly, the value of the marginal product of the second, third, fourth, and fifth workers are given, respectively, by Rs 120, Rs 90, Rs 60, and Rs 30. These numbers tell us how much the second, third, fourth, and fifth workers, respectively, are worth to the farmer. (The value of the marginal product is obtained by simply multiplying the marginal product with the price of the output.) Notice that, since the amount of land is held fixed, the value of the marginal product of labour is declining with the amount of labour employed by the farmer.

How would the marginal product of labour be affected if the amount of land were held fixed at a higher level, say at 2 hectares? Then, too, the marginal product of labour would decline as more labour is employed to work the land. The difference, however, is that, at each level of employment, the marginal product of a worker is higher now than when the amount of land was fixed at one hectare. (The marginal product of labour now is represented by the curve CD in Fig. 2.1.) This is because each worker has more land to work with than in the former case. This is an important point to grasp. The marginal product of one input increases when there is more of another input that is used in conjunction with it. The marginal product of land increases if more labour is employed on it. In industry, if capital and labour are used in conjunction to produce textiles, an increase in the amount of capital employed would usually raise the productivity of labour.

How does a farmer decide how much to pay for each input? He pays the prevailing rate. But how does this rate get determined in the market? This is an important question, because the answer determines the incomes received by the various people in the population. To answer this question, we need to understand the notion of perfectly competitive markets.

Competitive Markets and the Demand for Inputs

The essential feature of a perfectly competitive (or just *competitive*, for short) market is that every buyer and every seller is such an insignificant part of the market that no single individual can perceptibly influence the price of the product. Each economic agent is forced to simply take the price as given and beyond his control. Such markets typically obtain when there are very many buyers and sellers. A seller who quotes a price higher than the market price will find no buyers, because they can buy the product more cheaply from his competitors. A buyer who wants a product for less than the market price will find no willing sellers, because they would rather sell at the higher market price to other buyers.

We shall assume that all markets are competitive—not just the market for Grain and Textiles, but also the market for inputs like labour, land, capital, etc. Each economic agent, then, will take all prices as given and do the best he can to maximize his own well-being.

Let us see how producers in competitive markets decide on how much of an input to demand. Consider the farmer cultivating a plot of size one hectare in the example given above. Suppose the wage rate of an agricultural worker, as determined by the labour market, is Rs 60 a month. If the farmer takes this and the price of Grain (Rs 3 per kilogram) as given, how many workers would he want to hire in order to maximize his profits? As long as the income generated by a worker (i.e. the value of his marginal product) exceeds the wage he has to be paid, the farmer will find it profitable to employ him. So he will find it profitable to employ the first worker (who generates monthly revenues of Rs 150 but costs only Rs 60), the second worker, the third worker, and barely the fourth worker (who generates revenues exactly equal to his wages). He will not want to employ a fifth worker because he would add only Rs 30 a month to revenues, but cost the farmer Rs 60 a month. Thus a farmer will demand labour up until the value of the marginal product of the last worker hired is equal to the wage rate. A farmer's demand for labour will clearly depend upon the wage rate; the higher the wage rate, the fewer the workers demanded. If the wage rate was Rs 90 a month, the farmer will want no more than 3 workers. (Since all farmers face the same wage rate, the values of the marginal product of the last worker they each want to employ will be the same for all farmers.) By adding up the demand for labour from all farmers, we obtain the total demand for labour from the agricultural sector.

Equilibrium

In the above exercise we assumed that each farmer took the wage rate as given by the market. But how is this wage rate determined in the first place? In a competitive market, the wage rate is determined by the supply of and the demand for labour. Suppose, purely for the sake of argument, that there is a fixed supply of workers in agriculture. Also suppose that at the existing wage rate not all farmers can find enough workers to meet their demand for labour. In other words, suppose the value of the marginal product of labour is greater than the wage rate. In order to attract more workers, each farmer will try to bid them away from other farmers by offering higher wages. This process of competing for workers in this manner will ultimately increase the wage rate up until it is exactly equal to the value of the marginal product of labour. The wage rate will then settle down at this level because the demands of all farmers will be satisfied, i.e. their total demand for labour will be exactly equal to the supply of workers. This situation is referred to as a labour market *equilibrium* because there is no tendency for the wage rate to change. In equilibrium, the market is said to clear because there is no surplus of suppliers or of demanders. When the labour market clears, the wage rate will be equal to the value of the marginal product of labour.

What we have described above for labour will be equally true for all other inputs like land, capital (e.g. machines, plants), etc. Any input that is scarce in the sense that its marginal product is positive will command a price in the competitive market system. In equilibrium, the price of the input will be given by the value of its marginal product, and this price will be such that the total demand for the input from all producers will be exactly equal to its total supply from all owners. The price that an input commands in equilibrium will determine the income it yields to its owner. The incomes thus generated by the various inputs are then used by the people they accrue to for the purposes of demanding Grain and Textiles. It is important to understand the point that in competitive market equilibria, the payment for an input is equal to the value of its marginal product. In a market system, it is the productivity of an input that determines its income.

We must mention here that the supply of an input is not immutably fixed at a given point in time; it usually increases when the compensation it receives increases. Labour is an important example of this. If the wage rate is very low, workers may opt to work only a few hours a day and consume considerable amounts of leisure. As the wage rate increases, they may work more hours because now the income they forego by consuming leisure is higher. A higher wage, in other words, elicits a higher supply of labour. On the other hand, there are some inputs which are more or less immutably fixed in supply. Agricultural land is a good example. The same amount of land will be supplied to the market whether the rental price for a hectare of land is Rs 100 per month or Rs 0.10 per month, because agricultural land has no alternative uses—in contrast to a worker's time, which could be consumed as leisure. If, in equilibrium, an input which is in fixed supply commands a price because it is productive, the income that accrues to it is referred to as *rent*. The term rent is reserved for the income of an input, when the income is not necessary to elicit the total supply of the input that is offered to the market.

Let us now resume our discussion of equilibrium. The equilibrium prices of Grain and Textiles are also determined by demand and supply considerations. Suppose that at some price, the demand for Textiles from consumers exceeds the quantity supplied (i.e. there is *excess demand*). Then some consumers with purchasing power will not find the amount of Textiles they want. So they will be willing to offer higher prices to sellers. As the price rises, the total quantity demanded of Textiles will fall, thereby reducing the extent of the excess demand. This process will continue until the quantity demanded and quantity supplied are equal. At this point the Textile market is in equilibrium, i.e. the market clears. Suppose, on the other hand, that at some other price the supply of Textiles exceeds the demand (i.e. there is *excess supply*). Then some producers will be unable to find buyers for their wares, and so will cut prices to attract buyers. As the price falls, the total quantity demanded would increase, and the process will continue until the Textile market clears.

We see that whenever there is excess demand or excess supply in a market, there exist inexorable economic pressures which move the price in a direction so as to eliminate the excess demand or excess supply. In other words, the market is incessantly tending towards equilibrium. This is the attraction of the notion of market equilibrium. So if we are interested in knowing what the price of a good will be or how much of the good will be produced or bought, it is reasonable to determine these in the market equilibrium.

There is one important aspect of the competitive equilibrium that should be grasped. In order to meet consumers' demands, producers use the different resources available in the economy with an eye on their own profits; they operate purely out of self-interest. The prices adjust to ensure that the markets clear. When all markets are in equilibrium, it means that the resources of the economy have been allocated by the pricing mechanism to the various markets in order to ensure that demands are satisfied. But these demands reflect the tastes of the people comprising the society. It follows that the competitive market system, in equilibrium, allocates the economy's resources in such a way that the goods produced, and the quantities in which they are produced, are strictly according to the tastes of the people. No government, no central planner, or benevolent dictator is necessary to accomplish this; the decentralized market system brings this about of its own accord. As the economist Adam Smith emphasized over two hundred years ago, in a competitive market system the self-interest of producers is harnessed—as if by an Invisible Hand—to serve the tastes of society, even though this is not the intention of the producers.

After having grasped the principle of the Invisible Hand, it is equally important to be aware of another aspect of a market economy. It is true that the market system allocates resources to satisfy the tastes of the members of its society, as manifested by their demands. But, as we have seen, only those people who have purchasing power can register their demands in the market. The poor cannot, because they do not have the income to back their demands. Thus the allocation of resources in a market economy is biased in favour of the demands of the rich. It is for this reason that in many developing countries we see resources devoted to the production of luxury goods when substantial proportions of the populations are barely subsisting. If allocation of resources in the service of society by an Invisible Hand is the cardinal virtue of the competitive market system, its disregard for whom it caters to can be construed as its cardinal vice. Over long periods of time, there is no guarantee that economic development will equitably distribute the benefits of growth. Ensuring how growth can be rendered equitable is an important theme of this book.

3

The Basic Framework for a Closed Economy

In this chapter we set out to explain the workings of a simple model of a closed economy (one that is not open to international trade). In the next two chapters we will use this model to explain various aspects of Indian economic development over the past four decades. In comparison to many developing countries that have made substantial inroads into eradicating poverty, post-independence India has not engaged in a great deal of international trade. So a model that examines the character of economic development in a closed economy is not inappropriate for India. In subsequent chapters we shall examine the role trade can play in alleviating poverty.

Economic development can impinge differently on the well-being of different classes in an economy. Therefore, to facilitate our thinking it is important at the outset to group economic agents into broad classes, such that all members of a given class are similarly affected by the development process. A natural way to do this is to identify people by the manner in which they earn their income. Some earn only labour income; others earn only non-labour income, living off revenues generated by the assets they possess, like land; yet others earn both labour and non-labour income. Since it is best to begin with the simplest scenario, we shall assume here that there are only two economic classes: workers and landlords. We assume that there is only one kind of labour, namely unskilled labour. (We shall discuss the role of skills in a later chapter.) All people contribute labour, but not all people own land. We assume only a certain proportion of the population owns land. While we could have different landlords owning different amounts of land, it is conceptually simplest to assume that all landlords own identical amounts of land. Thus, in this model, there are two types of economic agents: workers who own no land and each of whom provides a fixed amount of labour, say one unit (however measured); and landlords each of whom owns a certain amount of land and provides one unit of labour.

In reality, the amount of labour a worker supplies is not immutably fixed; it would vary with the wage rate. The higher the wages of labour, the harder a worker would most likely work. If the compensation for work is very low, a worker may choose to consume more leisure. In a later chapter, this response of labour supply to the wage rate will play an important role. Since this is not the case here, we suppress it and assume that each agent provides a fixed amount of labour. The kind of goods that are produced in an economy and the amounts in which they are produced depend on what is demanded by those with purchasing power. We assume that the well-being of individuals in this economy is determined by the amounts consumed of two goods: Grain and Textiles. Recall that these goods are really proxies or representatives of two classes of goods: those produced by agriculture and those produced by industry. This simplification greatly facilitates thinking by enabling us to focus on the essence of the processes by which agriculture and industry contribute to economic development.

Let us first consider how much Grain and how much Textiles would be demanded by the population. The goods a consumer demands and the quantities in which she demands them will be determined not only by her tastes, but also her income. Incomes are determined in this economy by the competitve market system. We assume that all goods are sold in competitive markets, and that all the resources used as inputs (i.e. labour and land) are also hired in competitive markets. The wage rate for labour and the rental rate on land are then determined by the value of their marginal products, as explained in Chapter 2. Workers' income is comprised wholly of labour income, while landlords' income contains, in addition to this, revenues from renting out land. So no matter what the wage rate and the land rental rate are, landlords are always better off than workers.

We digress briefly here to explain the nature of the rental income from land to its owner. In this model, land is only used in agriculture. We saw in the last chapter that any scarce resource that contributes to the production of a valuable commodity will command a price in the market system. So potential cultivators will be willing to pay the landlord a certain annual fee (the rental rate) for use of the land, which accrues as rental income to the landlord. But what if the landlord cultivates his own land, instead of renting it out? Then, too, the land he owns will yield him an income of precisely the same amount, even though he may not call it rental income. This is why.

Suppose a one-hectare plot of land is to be cultivated with a single worker's labour. Suppose the value of the output produced is Rs 1,500 a year, and the values of the marginal products of labour and land are Rs 500 per year and Rs 1,000 per year, respectively. The landlord who owns a hectare of land has several options open to him with regard to *how* he earns his income. One option would be for him to sell his labour services in the labour market and to rent out his land to some other cultivator. In this case, he earns a labour income of Rs 500 a year (the value of the marginal product of labour) and a rental income from land of Rs 1,000 (the value of the marginal product of land). His total annual income is Rs 1,500. Another option open to the landlord is for him to cultivate his land himself, using his own labour. In this case, he gets to keep as income the entire value of the output, which is Rs 1,500 per year. So in both cases he earns the same total income. In the second option, however, he must attribute or impute to his labour a contribution of Rs 500 and to land a contribution of Rs 1,000 because these are the payments that the landlord would receive for his labour and land, respectively, in competitive markets. In other words, the contribution to his income from his ownership of land is the same in both cases; the only difference is that in the first case it is explicit, while in the second it is implicit. This contribution is what is referred to as land rental income, whether or not the owner actually rents out the land. It is useful for us to explicitly separate out these two components of a landlord's income because some economic events impinge differently on wage income and land rental income.

We have seen in the last chapter that the demand for various goods by individuals will be determined, among other things, by their tastes. Since food is much more essential for survival than Textiles, we argued in the last chapter that it is reasonable to suppose that tastes are hierarchical. In other words, until an individual's consumption of Grain is sufficiently high, say G kilograms, the individual will spend all of his income on Grain. Once Grain consumption reaches G kilograms, the individual spends all of the remaining income on Textiles. If an individual's income is very low, he may not be able to consume G kilograms of Grain despite having exhausted all of his income on Grain.

Suppose, for example, G is 20 and the price of Grain is Rs 5 per kilogram. Then an individual, Ahmed, who has an income of Rs 75 a month will want to spend it all on food and thus consume 15 kilograms of Grain a month. Another individual, Biswas, with an income of Rs 150 a month will want to spend Rs 100 a month on Grain, thereby consuming 20 kilograms of Grain a month, and spend the remaining Rs 50 on Textiles, i.e. on industrial products. Suppose the price of Textiles is Rs 25 a metre. Then Biswas will want to purchase 2 metres of textiles. Yet another individual, Cherian, with an income of Rs 300 per month will want to purchase 20 kilograms of Grain and 8 metres of Textiles. At the prices Rs 5 per kilogram for Grain and Rs 25 per metre for Textiles, the *demands* of Ahmed, Biswas, and Cherian for Grain and Textiles will be 15 kilograms and 0 metres, 20 kilograms and 2 metres, and 20 kilograms and 8 metres, respectively.

The simple example presented above illustrates two points. First, since food is essential for survival, tastes are constructed in such a way that income is first allocated to the agricultural good and then, if income is left over, to the industrial good. Thus people with very low incomes will purchase only Grain; they will demand no Textiles. It is only people who are sated with food who demand industrial goods. It follows that as individuals get richer their demands for agricultural and industrial goods do not increase proportionately. In the above example, Cherian's income is twice that of Biswas but his demands for Grain and Textiles are not twice as large. In fact, Cherian demands the same amount of Grain as Biswas but four times as much Textiles. If an individual who is already sated with food at the current income level becomes richer, he will spend all of his increase in income on Textiles. As an economy develops, if all the people get richer and richer, a stage will come when most of the increases in income will be used to demand more industrial goods.

There is a second point to note, which is crucial to what follows. Suppose in the above example everything is as before but the price of Textiles changes. Say, due to technological progress in the industrial sector the price of Textiles drops from Rs 25 per metre to Rs 20 per metre. Thus Textiles have become cheaper relative to Grain. (Previously 5 kilograms of Grain were required in exchange for 1 metre of Textiles, and now only 4 kilograms of Grain are needed.) How do the demands of Ahmed, Biswas, and Cherian change in response to the change in the relative price? As before, since Ahmed's income is only Rs 75, he will want to spend it all on food and demand 15 kilograms of Grain; the fact that Textiles are now cheaper relative to Grain will not induce him to switch some expenditure away from food, in favour of industrial goods. Biswas, who was previously sated with food, will still demand 20 kilograms of Grain, and with the remaining Rs 50, he will demand 2.5 metres of Textiles. Likewise, Cherian will demand only 20 kilograms of Grain as before, and with the remaining Rs 200 he will demand 10 metres of Textiles. In other words, the demands for Grain coming from the people who are not yet sated with Grain *and* from the people who are remain unchanged following the decrease in the price of Textiles. When tastes are hierarchical, people do not substitute Grain for Textiles as one becomes cheaper relative to the other. They will not curtail expenditure on one good in order to spend more on a cheaper good. If they end up buying more of the latter, it is simply because a given income enables them to buy more of the good when it is cheaper.

In a closed market economy, the goods that are demanded must be produced by the economy. So we now turn from the demand side to the supply side of the economy. Since individuals demand at most only two goods, Grain and Textiles, there will be only two sectors: an agricultural sector and an industrial sector. We describe below the technologies that are used in these sectors to produce the goods.

The industrial sector of the economy uses only one input to produce Textiles, namely labour. A fixed number of man-hours is required to produce one metre of Textiles. This number characterizes the productivity of the technology. An improvement in the technology would mean fewer man-hours of labour are required to produce one metre of Textiles. Equivalently, one man-hour of labour would produce more Textiles than it did before.

The agricultural sector uses two inputs to produce Grain: land and labour. The technology is such that if we double the amount of land and labour, the output of Grain will double. (The total output from two identical plots of land, using identical amounts of labour, will clearly be twice as high as the output from one.) By an increase in agricultural productivity we shall mean that more output can be produced with the same amount of land and labour. Equivalently, proportionately less land and labour will be required to produce one kilogram of Grain.

The total amount of land in the economy is fixed and this input is used only in agriculture. One difference between land and labour is that, since labour is used in agriculture and in industry, the amount of labour applied to agriculture is variable. This is a crucial difference between the industrial and agricultural sectors: industry, in this simple model, uses only one input (labour), and that input is completely variable; agriculture uses two inputs (land and labour), but one of them is fixed.

One important implication follows from the above-mentioned difference. Since there are no fixed inputs in industry, every additional worker applied to producing Textiles increases the output of that sector by a constant amount, determined by the productivity of the technology. In other words, the marginal product of a worker (i.e. increase in output generated by a worker) is constant, and independent of the number of workers employed in industry. In agriculture, however, the situation is different. Since the amount of land is fixed, as more and more labour is applied to agriculture, ultimately there must be diminishing returns to labour as we saw in the previous chapter. The increase in output contributed by each additional worker is less than the contribution of the previous worker. In other words, the marginal product of a worker declines as more and more workers are allocated to agriculture. This arises because each worker has less and less land to work with as the total employment in agriculture is increased. If the amount of labour in agriculture increases, the total output (or product) of Grain from the sector will undoubtedly increase, but this will be accompanied by a declining marginal product of labour. The same process will work in reverse when labour is withdrawn from agriculture. If fewer and fewer workers remain in agriculture, the total output of the sector would decline, but the marginal product of each worker would rise.

The importance of diminishing returns in agriculture stems from the fact that in a competitive market economy, the wage rate of a worker is determined by the worth of his marginal product. If economic development is to make a dent on poverty, the wage rate must rise because the landless workers are the poorest class in the economy. But for the wage rate to rise the marginal product of a worker in agriculture must rise. If the technology in agriculture is stagnant, the only way this can happen is by labour being drawn away from agriculture into industry. This is the reason why in countries that have developed and become richer, the industrial sector has regularly employed a larger and larger proportion of the work force. This is what ought to happen in any developing country. But there is nothing automatic about this process, as we shall see. Why this process has been sabotaged in India is a major theme of this book.

In the argument above, we have taken the wage rate of a worker as being determined by the value of his marginal product in agriculture. Why not by the value of his marginal product in industry, since we are assuming that all workers have identical skills? It does not matter which we choose, because under conditions of perfect competition the two must be identical, in equilibrium. To see this, suppose the prices of Grain and Textiles are Rs 5 a kilogram and Rs 25 a metre, respectively. Also suppose the marginal product of a worker is 10 kilograms of Grain a month in agriculture and 3 metres of Textiles per month in industry. Since under conditions of perfect competition a worker will be offered a wage equal to the value of his marginal product, workers in industry will earn Rs 75 a month, while workers in agriculture will receive only Rs 50. This situation cannot be sustained because workers in agriculture will move to industry, offer to work for slightly less than Rs 75 a month, and still be better off than they were in agriculture. The exodus of labour from agriculture will increase the marginal product of labour in that sector. The transfer of labour will continue until the marginal product of labour in agriculture rises to 15 kilograms per month. At this point the reallocation of labour stops because the value of the marginal product of labour is Rs 75 a month in both sectors.

In other words, the competitive process ensures that workers with the same skill earn the same wage in all sectors of the economy. (Unions in the industrial sector can, and do, prevent this from happening. We shall have something to say about this in a later chapter. Incorporating the role of unions at this stage, by departing from our assumption of competitve markets, would prematurely complicate the analysis.)

We have discussed separately the demand and supply sides of an economy in which the population is interested in consuming two representative goods: Grain and Textiles. We are now ready to put the two sides together to examine precisely how the market economy will allocate its resources (land and labour) in order to produce the goods desired, in the amounts desired. We shall also see how the incomes of workers and landlords are determined, and how the prices of Grain and Textiles get set. Once this is understood, we will be in a position to investigate how progress in the industrial or the agricultural sectors will impinge on the well-being of the two classes.

In putting together the demand and supply sides of the economy, let us recall that as economic agents, individuals play a dual role. On the production side, they are suppliers of the inputs (land and labour) used to produce the goods. The total payment they receive for the inputs they supply is their income. On the demand side, they are consumers; they use their incomes to demand various amounts of the goods, as dictated by their tastes and the prices of the goods. Since goods are produced to meet the demands of people, it is they, as economic agents, who form the link between demand and supply.

To see how the economy we have described would allocate its resources, suppose we begin with some arbitrary prices for Grain and Textiles, and an arbitrary allocation of labour between the two sectors. (Since land is of use only in agriculture, all of it will be allocated to that sector.) The amount of labour used in the industrial sector will determine the amount of Textiles produced by that sector. The amount of labour used in the agricultural sector, together with the amount of land in the economy, will determine the amount of Grain produced by that sector. In other words, once the resource allocation is given, the outputs are immediately determined. Now the allocation of labour determines the value of the marginal product of labour in the two sectors, and also the value of the marginal product of land. These, we have seen, are nothing but the wage rate of labour and the rental rate of land, respectively, under competitive market conditions. These, in turn, determine the incomes accruing to workers and to landlords. Now each individual uses his income to manifest a demand for Grain and, possibly, for Textiles. So once the income of each economic agent is determined, so is the total demand for Grain and Textiles. What guarantee is there that the total demand for Grain by the population will be equal to the amount of Grain supplied by the agricultural sector, or that the total demand for Textiles will be equal to the amount of Textiles supplied by the industrial sector? For an arbitary allocation of labour across the sectors, there is no guarantee, whatsoever, that the markets will clear.

When demands and supplies in any sector are unequal in a market economy a whole chain of processes is called into operation which tends to bring about equality. There exist compelling economic forces which will relentlessly reallocate resources in such a manner that supply will diminish in a sector where the output exceeds demand, and increase in a sector where output falls short of demand. To see this, suppose the supply of Grain falls short of demand. Let us trace the effects of this. Since the demand for Grain exceeds the supply, it means that some people with purchasing power cannot get as much Grain as they would like. This situation is not likely to repeat itself period after period. For, these people with unsatisfied food demand will offer sellers higher prices for their Grain, and sellers will gladly oblige. An excess demand for Grain, therefore, will end up increasing the price of Grain. This will increase the value of the marginal product of labour in agriculture and, hence, the wage rate in agriculture. Some workers in industry will quit their jobs and seek employment in agriculture, because the latter now offers a higher wage. The increase in employment in agriculture results in an increase in the output of Grain, thereby tending to eliminate the excess demand and bring about market clearance.

What ultimately brings a halt to the transfer of labour from industry to agriculture in the above process? It is diminishing returns to labour in agriculture. As more and more labour is employed in agriculture, the marginal product of a worker and, hence, the wage offered to a worker in agriculture will decrease.

Ultimately, the gap between the wages of industrial and agricultural workers (which was created by the rise in the price of Grain) will be eliminated. At this point, the reallocation of resources stops. The process described above will work in reverse when there is excess supply in a market.

The argument given above implicitly assumed that when there was excess demand for Grain (which attracted resources into that sector) there was excess supply in the Textiles sector (which could accommodate the agricultural sector's need for more resources). What would have happened if there was excess demand in both sectors? Such an occurrence is impossible; an excess demand in one sector will necessarily be accompanied with an excess supply in the other, and vice versa. A situation in which there is excess demand or excess supply in both sectors can never arise. Here is the reason why. Suppose the value of the total output of Grain is Rs 2,000. Of this, let us say labour's contribution (as measured by the value of its marginal product) is Rs 1,200, and land's is Rs 800. Competitive markets will ensure that these will accrue as incomes to agricultural labour and land, respectively. Suppose the value of the total output of Textiles is Rs 1,000. Since labour is the only input used to produce Textiles, the income accruing to industrial workers will be Rs 1,000. The value of the output of the economy (= Rs 2,000 + Rs 1,000) is exactly equal to the total income generated in the economy (= Rs 1,200 + Rs 800 + Rs 1,000).

This is as it must be because the income of an input used in any sector is really the claim it has on the output of that sector. The sum total of the claims (which is the total income) cannot exceed or fall short of the total value of a closed economy's output. Now if, as consumers, workers, and landlords demand Rs 2,000 worth of Grain and Rs 1,000 worth of Textiles, both markets will be in equilibrium, because these are precisely the values of the outputs of the two sectors. Suppose, instead, that the consumers demand Rs 2,500 worth of Grain. Then there will be excess demand in the Grain market. Since the remaining income is Rs 500, consumers can only demand Rs 500 worth of Textiles. There will necessarily be excess supply in the Textiles market. If there is too much purchasing power seeking too little output in one sector (leading to excess demand), the reverse must necessarily be true elsewhere.

We thus see that in a competitive market economy, powerful

economic forces exist that will tend to bring about equality between demand and supply in every sector of the economy. When
markets clear in all sectors, we say the economy is in
general equilibrium. The situation is an *equilibrium* in the sense that
there is no tendency for resources to move across the sectors or
for any price to change, which is so because there is neither excess demand nor excess supply anywhere. It is *general* in the
sense that the equilibrium encompasses the entire economy with
all sectors and their mutual interactions included. The essence of
economic analysis that is general equilibrium in nature is that it
captures the interactions between sectors, and does not merely
look at one sector in isolation. In reality, changes in one sector
spill over into other sectors and induce changes there, which in
turn spill over into the original sector, and so on. Unintended
consequences of economic policies are invariably a result of the
accompanying economic analyses not being sufficiently general
equilibrium in nature. At the heart of the process of economic
development for a country at India's stage of development is the
interaction between the agricultural and industrial sectors. Thus
an understanding of how resources get allocated, incomes determined and equilibrium attained in such an economy is imperative. To ensure this, we present below a simple numerical
example and work through the logic of general equilibrium. (The
numbers used in the example are not meant to be realistic; they
have been chosen so as to keep the arithmetic simple. This allows
us to concentrate on the economic logic of the process by which
an economy arrives at equilibrium.)

Consider a simple economy comprising one hundred individuals, seventy-five of whom are landless and the other twenty-five own one hectare of land each. The marginal product of
labour in industry is 5 metres of Textiles per worker per month,
and is independent of the number of workers employed in industry (i.e. there are no diminishing returns). In agriculture, the
marginal product of labour declines with employment. Suppose
that initially the price of Grain and Textiles are Rs 3 per kilogram
and Rs 12 per metre, respectively. Also suppose that labour has
been arbitrarily allocated across the sectors: there are 15 people
working in agriculture and 85 in industry. The total output of
agriculture (i.e. its supply) is 600 kilograms of Grain and the
marginal product of labour is 20 kilograms per month. The total

output of industry (i.e. its supply) is 425 metres of Textiles per month. The marginal product of land is 12 kilograms of Grain per month. Finally, assume that an individual gets satiated with Grain only after he consumes 20 kilograms a month. The question we now ask is whether the situation just spelled out is an equilibrium for the economy.

To answer this question, we have to see if demand equals supply for Grain and Textiles. But because demands depend on people's incomes, we first have to compute their incomes. In agriculture, each worker's marginal product is 20 kilograms of Grain per month and each kilogram of Grain is worth Rs 3. So the value of an agricultural worker's marginal product is Rs 3 x 20 = Rs 60 per month. In industry, the marginal product of a worker is 5 metres of Textiles per month, and each metre is worth Rs 12. So the value of an industrial worker's marginal product is Rs 12 x 5 = Rs 60 per month. Since a worker's wages are given by the value of his marginal product, workers in both sectors will earn an income of Rs 60 per month. A landlord will earn, in addition to this, rental income from the one hectare of land he owns. Since the marginal product of land is 12 kilograms of Grain, this rental income is Rs 3 x 12 = Rs 36 per month. Thus a landlord's total income is Rs 96 per month.

We can now determine how much of each good a worker and a landlord would demand. Each worker's income of Rs 60 would enable him to demand 20 kilograms of Grain (= Rs 60 ÷ Rs 3/kilogram), leaving him just about sated with Grain but with no income left over to demand Textiles. Each landlord will want to spend Rs 60 to purchase 20 kilograms of Grain and with the remaining Rs 36 he will demand 3 metres of Textiles (= Rs 36 ÷ Rs 12/metre). The total demand for Grain from the entire economy will be 100 x 20 kilograms = 2,000 kilograms, and the total demand for Textiles will be 25 x 3 metres = 75 metres. But the agricultural sector's supply of Grain is 600 kilograms, and the industrial sector's supply of Textiles is 425 metres. Thus there is an excess demand for Grain and an excess supply of Textiles. The assumed allocation of resources, therefore, cannot be an equilibrium.

What would we expect to happen in the above situation? Producers of Textiles, seeing that not all their output is being sold, will cut prices. This will reduce the value of the marginal product of industrial workers and, hence, the wage they are offered. Farmers, on the other hand, will see the price of Grain go up, because their output falls short of demand. This will increase the worth of labour in agriculture and, hence, will push up the wages offered in that sector. Thus we will witness an exodus of labour from industry into agriculture, thereby eliminating the excess supply of Textiles and the excess demand for Grain.

Suppose that after the adjustment described above has taken place, the situation is as follows. The price of Grain is Rs 5 per kilogram and that of Textiles is Rs 10 per metre. There are 62.5 people working in agriculture and only 37.5 in industry. (This means 62 people are working full-time in agriculture and 37 working full-time in industry, and one person is working half-time in each sector. The total output of Grain is 1250 kilograms and the marginal product of a worker in agriculture is 10 kilograms per worker, while that of land is 25 kilograms per hectare. The output of Textiles is 187.5 metres. Mimicking the steps followed in the paragraphs above, we can easily see that a worker's income is now Rs 50 per month, while a landlord's is Rs 175 per month. At the new prices, a worker would demand 10 kilograms of Grain and no Textiles. A landlord would demand 20 kilograms of Grain and 7.5 metres of Textiles. The total demand for Grain in the economy is 1,250 kilograms, and for Textiles it is 187.5 metres of Textiles. Since these are precisely equal to their corresponding supplies, we see that the economy now is in general equilibrium.

In the equilibrium of the example given above, the workers are consuming only Grain, while landlords, being richer than workers, are consuming both Grain and Textiles. If the population of the economy were lower, and the amount of land remained unchanged, workers would be better off and perhaps they, too, would be buying Textiles in equilibrium. This is because fewer workers in agriculture implies a larger marginal product for labour; each worker has more land to work with and hence is more productive. Thus the land-to-labour ratio is an important determinant of the well-being of landless workers, the poorest class in the economy. This ratio is one fundamental avenue through which overpopulation in India impinges on the poverty of its masses. We shall discuss this at greater length in a subsequent chapter.

4

The Importance of Technological Progress in Agriculture

In this chapter, we investigate why technological progress in agriculture is crucial to the well-being of the poorest class. Using the model that was set out in the last chapter, we demonstrate why a neglect of the agricultural sector in favour of the industrial sector has very dire consequences in terms of poverty alleviation. In the economic development of a closed economy, there is a particular sequence in which technological progress in the two sectors should be emphasized: initially, agriculture should be given precedence over industry. To reverse the sequence and give priority to industry first is counter-productive. If resources are diverted to industry, leaving agriculture stagnant and backward, this very backwardness of agriculture will undermine industry's potential contribution to the goal of poverty alleviation. If the people below the poverty line—who constitute over a third of the Indian population—are not to be left out from sharing the fruits of economic growth, the technology in the agricultural sector should have achieved a certain minimum level of productivity. We demonstrate in this and the next chapter, that only after this minimum level has been achieved, can we reasonably expect industrial progress to benefit all economic classes of the population.

The issue of the precedence that agriculture should be given over industry in the initial stages of economic development is a crucial one for India. Like most of the colonies that were freed after the Second World War, India set about rapidly industrializing, seeing this as a way of quickly catching up with Western standards of living. The Second Five Year Plan (1956–61) explicitly implemented this strategy for India. As a consequence, agriculture suffered from benign neglect. On the face of it, such a strategy may seem entirely reasonable. After all, judging from the example of the developed countries, economic development has been almost synonymous with industrialization. In most developed countries like the United States, England, and Canada, for example, only about four or five per cent of the population is engaged in agriculture. (And far from importing their food requirements, many, in fact, are exporters of food.) So it might seem entirely reasonable to conclude that a developing country aspiring to the living standards of the developed countries should not devote resources to a sector that will ultimately employ an insignificant proportion of the population. It is the burden of this chapter to explain, among other things, why this conclusion is an error, and a grievous error at that.

Before we begin our analysis, let us consider what exactly is meant by the term 'technical progress' or 'technological progress'. Suppose that, given the existing state of knowledge (which is what is embodied in a technology), a combination of 5 workers and 10 hectares of land produces 200 kilograms of Grain. For this input combination, suppose the marginal product of labour is 20 kilograms of Grain per worker and that of land is 10 kilograms of Grain per hectare. This means that if the amount of land were held fixed at 10 hectares and one more worker was employed, the output of Grain would increase by 20 kilograms. If, on the other hand, the amount of labour used were fixed at 5 workers and one more hectare was brought into cultivation, the output of Grain would increase by 10 kilograms. Now suppose the state of knowledge relevant for agricultural production improves and, as a result, the same input combination of 5 workers and 10 hectares of land generates an output of 220 kilograms of Grain. Also suppose the marginal products of labour and land increase.

Since more output (ten per cent more, in this example, can now be produced from a given combination of inputs, we say technical (or technological) progress has taken place in agriculture. Equivalently, a given amount of output can now be produced with less labour and/or less land than before. In other words, technological progress helps us economize on scarce inputs.

When the production technology uses more than one input, as

here, an issue arises which is best clarified right away. It is conceivable that technological progress impinges unevenly on the marginal productivities of labour and land. If the productivity of labour increases by more than that of land, then the technical change offers greater scope to save on labour, i.e. it is biased in favour of labour. Likewise, the technical change is biased in favour of land if it raises the productivity of land by more than that of labour. While technical change, by its very nature, effectively renders inputs more abundant, biased technical change renders one input relatively more abundant than the other. We will restrict ourselves, in this chapter and in the entire book, to technical change that increases the marginal productivities of both inputs in the same proportion, i.e. it is *neutral* in the sense that it is not biased in favour of either input. By rendering both labour and land relatively more abundant in the same proportion, the technical change considered here does not, by itself, put workers at a disadvantage relative to landowners, or vice versa. If the technical change is neutral in this sense, the marginal productivities of labour and land in the above example would rise, respectively, to 22 kilograms per worker and 11 kilograms per hectare, each ten per cent higher than before.

We are now ready to consider how productivity increases in agriculture, induced by technical change, will impinge on the well-being of the population. As in the last chapter, consider an economy which comprises a given population, some proportion of which owns land. Each individual has hierarchical tastes, and demands Textiles only after he has consumed, say, G kilograms of Grain. In the conceptual exercise to be conducted below we shall deliberately hold fixed the number of man-hours required to produce one metre of Textiles, i.e. technology is assumed not to change in industry. This enables us to isolate the effects of agricultural productivity increases.

Let us begin with a situation in which the agricultural technology is extremely primitive. This means that the marginal products of labour and land are very low, and so a great deal of labour and land are required to produce a kilogram of Grain. Since food is uppermost in the hierarchy of tastes, it follows that a primitive agricultural technology will force all the economy's labour into agriculture. For when people have very low productivity, every available person in the economy will be required to

produce food. There will be, then, only an agricultural sector in
the economy. Since landlords are richer than workers, however,
they will necessarily get to consume more Grain than the landless workers.

Now suppose agricultural productivity increases because better and better technologies become available. At each level of
agricultural productivity, there will be incomes accruing to
workers and landlords, as determined by the marginal products
of labour and land. These incomes determine the quantities of
Grain and Textiles demanded. If the economy is in equilibrium,
the quantities demanded must be equal to their respective quantities supplied. Associated with the equilibrium, there will be a
level of Grain and Textiles consumption for each economic agent
in the economy. When agricultural productivity changes due to
technical progress, the marginal products and, hence, the quantities demanded and quantities supplied, will all change and the
economy will settle down at a new equilibrium. The graphs in
the upper and lower panels of Fig. 4.1 indicate the consumptions,
in equilibrium, of Grain and Textiles by landlords and workers at
various levels of agricultural productivity. It is important to realize that at each level of agricultural productivity, the economy is
in a different equilibrium.

Let us try to understand Fig. 4.1. In a competitive labour
market, workers earn a wage given by the value of their marginal product. So when their productivity increases, so do their
incomes—which they spend exclusively on food at this stage.
Thus the Grain consumption of workers will increase with increases in productivity in agriculture, as shown in the figure.
Now the rental rate on land is given, in a competitive land
market, by the value of its marginal product. So when agricultural productivity increases, the rental component of a landlord's
income also increases. Thus a landlord, who also earns labour income, will see his total income (and, therefore, his Grain consumption) rise faster than a worker's. This is why, in the upper
panel of Fig. 4.1, the profile representing a landlord's Grain consumption is steeper than that representing a worker's. Thus,
starting from a primitive state, an increase in agricultural
productivity unambiguously makes both landlords and workers
better off, although at different rates.

From the upper panel of Fig. 4.1 we see that when the agricul-

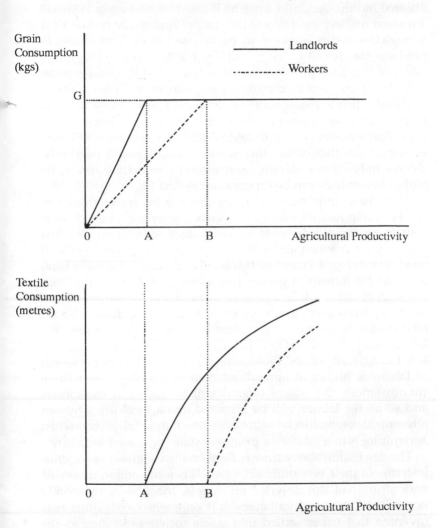

FIG. 4.1 *Illustrates how the grain and textile consumption of landlords and workers change when agricultural productivity increases.*

tural productivity level is OA, the Grain consumption of a landlord is precisely G kilograms, i.e., he is sated with Grain. What happens when the productivity increases beyond OA? The landlord's income increases, but he will not spend any of his ad-

ditional income on Grain since he is sated; he will want to spend
it instead on Textiles. The productivity of agriculture is now high
enough for some workers to be released from agriculture to
produce the Textiles demanded by the landlords. The lower
panel of Fig. 4.1 represents an individual's Textiles consumption
in terms of the level of productivity in agriculture. We see that a
landlord's Textile consumption is zero until agricultural productivity is OA, and increases thereafter. A worker's Textiles consumption remains zero until agricultural productivity is OB, and
then increases thereafter. Since workers, in contrast to landlords,
receive only labour income, agricultural productiviy has to be
higher before they can begin consuming Textiles.

There is an important inference that can be drawn from Fig.
4.1. For an industrial sector to be viable, there must be a class of
consumers (landlords here) which is sated with Grain. But this
can only occur when agricultural productivity is above a critical
level (OA in Fig. 4.1). Below this level of productivity, there is no
demand for industrial goods, tastes being what they are. From
the supply side, a low agricultural productivity means all the
economy's resources are required to feed the population. So no
labour can be released for industrial production. Competitive
labour markets will ensure that this is so through the wage offered in agriculture and (potentially) in industry. Since the worth
of labour is higher in agriculture than in industry under these
circumstances, the wages offered will be higher in the former
and so all the labour will be attracted into agriculture. Thus an
attempt at prematurely setting up an industrial sector when
agriculture is in a relatively primitive state is doomed to failure.

The discussion above throws light on the evolution of societies
in terms of their economic activities. When the notion of settled
agriculture had not dawned on people, tribes were essentially
nomadic hunters and gatherers. It is only when agriculture was
invented that tribes settled into stable societies. As long as the
agricultural technologies were primitive, these societies
remained agrarian. It is only in societies with relatively advanced
technologies for producing food that we observe substantial
levels of economic activities that are divorced from agriculture.

No single event has contributed more to the rapid economic
growth experienced by the now-developed countries as the Industrial Revolution that took place in England in the latter half of

the eighteenth century. Economic historians have debated at length on the issue of why England, and not a country like France on the European continent, was the first to experience the Industrial Revolution. While many pertinent reasons have been suggested, one important reason has to do with the fact that English agriculture was much more productive than French agriculture. Around 1750, about 60 per cent of the French population was employed in agriculture while only about 45 per cent of the English population was thus employed. At the time, neither country was importing significant amounts of food. It follows that English agriculture was 25 per cent more productive, since a much smaller proportion of the population working in agriculture could sustain the entire population. These facts are consistent with what we have said above regarding the need for efficient agriculture in order to sustain a robust industrial sector.

When the agricultural productivity is at a level OA and OB in Fig. 4.1, the demand for Textiles comes only from the landlords. Any increase in productivity increases their demand for Textiles, but not Grain. Since fewer workers are needed to meet the economy's food demand, the productivity increase releases labour from agriculture. Thus the emerging demand for Textiles will be met by a corresponding supply from the industrial sector, which now employs the workers released from agriculture. Thus beyond OA, agriculture will employ less and less of the labour force. At productivity level OB, even workers get sated with Grain. Higher incomes, generated by further increases in productivity, will translate exclusively into higher Textile demands. Thus beyond OB, technical progress in agriculture will release labour even more rapidly for industry.

We have pointed out earlier that in the developed countries of the West, only a small proportion (less than five per cent) of the population is employed in agriculture. That so small a proportion can provide the food necessary to support the entire population bears testimony to the incredibly high levels of agricultural productivities in these countries. The high proportion of the labour force employed in industry is an *effect* of a highly developed agricultural sector, not an independent *cause* of economic development. To look at the proportions of the population employed in industry and agriculture in developed countries and to infer from them that agriculture is relatively unimportant in the development process is to draw a wrong and unwarranted conclusion. The analysis we have presented above shows that this error comes from confusing cause and effect.

Until the agricultural productivity level is sufficiently high (OB in Fig. 4.1), an increase in productivity makes both classes better off. After it has reached OB, further increases in productivity continue to make workers unambiguously better off. It is possible though not inevitable, however, that landlords may become worse off now. The reason for this is not hard to see. Once the productivity level reaches OB, all the people in the economy are sated with food. So as the economy gets richer, the quantity of Grain demanded from agriculture will remain constant. Therefore, in equilibrium, the quantity of Grain supplied will have to be constant. But we have seen that it is in the nature of technical progress that it effectively renders inputs more abundant (i.e. less scarce) by reducing the inputs required to produce a kilogram of Grain. Thus, for the purpose of producing the fixed amount of food required by the population, continued technical progress will render the economy's agricultural land less and less scarce an input. So the economic value of land will decline and, hence, the rent on a hectare of land will decline.

We can see the above point in a different manner. Beyond productivity level OB, all increases in demand are for Textiles only. Since there is a fixed demand for Grain and a potentially higher supply of Grain made possible by the technical progress, the price of Grain must fall relative to the price of Textiles. In other words, the value of the marginal product of land must fall and, with that, so must the rental rate on land. The rental income component of a landlord's income will necessarily decline. But, in spite of this, landlords may still be better off because, in our model, they also earn a labour income, which necessarily increases. If landlords did not work and simply lived off the rental income from land, they would be unambiguously worse off when agricultural productivity increases beyond OB.

It might be objected that the asymmetric effects of agricultural productivity increase on labour and land rental incomes claimed above are not possible. After all, we have assumed at the outset that the technological progress we consider is neutral in that it increases the marginal productivities of land and labour in the same proportion. So, it might be argued, if the fall in the price of

Grain following the technical progress is so steep that it decreases the value of the marginal product of land, then it must also reduce the value of the marginal product of labour. So if land rents fall, so must wages. This argument is incorrect, and for the following, revealing reason.

Suppose the productivity in agriculture is at some level beyond OB in Fig. 4.1. Suppose that in the associated equilibrium, there are 6 workers employed in agriculture, working 10 hectares of land, the total amount of agricultural land in the economy. The output of this sector is equal, in equilibrium, to the quantity demanded. Now if there is technical progress that is neutral, it is true, by definition, that the marginal productivities of labour and land will increase proportionately—*if* the amount of labour used with the 10 hectares of land is held fixed at 6 workers. But in point of fact, the allocation of labour between agriculture and industry cannot remain the same in the new equilibrium as in the old. If it did, the supply of Grain with the superior technology would exceed the quantity demanded (which stays the same as before). The only way excess supply can be avoided is by an exodus of labour from agriculture. The reduction in the amount of labour employed in agriculture with a given amount of land further increases the marginal product of labour—reinforcing the effect of the technical progress on labour's productivity. The situation with land, however, is different. In the new equilibrium, there is less labour working the land than in the old equilibrium. This lowers the marginal product of land—countering the effect of the technical progress on land's productivity. Thus, although the technical progress in agriculture has treated labour and land in a neutral fashion, after the reallocation of labour induced by the technical progress has taken place, the marginal productivity of labour increases by a higher proportion than does land's. It is for this reason that, even with a fall in the price of Grain, the value of the marginal product of labour is higher than before, while that of land is lower.

At the heart of the potentially asymmetric effects of agricultural productivity increases on labour and land is the fact that the scope of economic activities the two inputs can engage in is different. Labour has uses in both the sectors, while land has uses only in one. If technical progress in agriculture releases labour from that sector, it is because the demand for Grain is not rising

as fast as supply can. The demand for Grain does not rise as
rapidly because, beyond productivity level OA in Fig. 4.1, people
choose to spend some or all of their increases in income on Textiles—which require labour to produce. In other words, when
technological progress releases labour from agriculture, it simultaneously creates a demand for labour elsewhere, i.e. in industry.
The same thing does not happen for land, since land is of little
use in industry. Even as land is being rendered less and less
scarce in agriculture by technological progress, this input has no
option but to remain in that sector. Herein lies the asymmetry between land and labour *vis–a–vis* agriculture.

The potentially damaging consequences to farmers of technical progress in agriculture when the state of the technology is already advanced is one reason why there are price supports for
agricultural products in most developed countries. Despite the
fact that only an insignificant fraction of the population is
employed in agriculture in these countries, agricultural technology is so advanced that, in the absence of price supports and
various subsidies, farmers' incomes would be very low relative
to those in industry. The fact that most developed countries
protect their agricultural sectors is evidence of the effectiveness
of farmers' lobbies in persuading their respective governments of
the helplessness of their condition. This is also the fundamental
reason why the protection of the agricultural sectors was one of
the most contentious issues in the recent Uruguay round of the
General Agreement of Tariffs and Trade (GATT) talks.

While what has been said in the above paragraph pertains to
developed countries, it is not entirely without relevance for less
developed countries like India. Technological progress in agriculture will initially improve the standard of living of the landed
class (i.e. the landowners), but it will ultimately work to their
detriment. If landed farmers do not collectively organize and
lobby for government intervention, the inexorable force of competition will ensure a decline in their incomes relative to those in
industry. Thus landed farmers have an incentive to organize, but
this is made difficult by the large numbers involved and their
geographic dispersion. Despite these difficulties, there are
reasonably effective farmers' lobbies in India. When such lobbies
emerge, they push for price supports for their products and other
subsidies (like the massive one for fertilizers). They tend to be

less enthusiastic about lobbying the government to sponsor productivity-enhancing projects like irrigation. It is in the individual interest of a farmer to have greater access to a steady supply of water, for example, when agricultural productivity rises. But if the productivity increase is diffused throughout the sector, the effect on farmers' incomes can be devastating. The individual interests of landed farmers are here opposed to their collective interests. Workers, however, benefit in both cases, though not necessarily to the same extent. (An increase in the price of Grain because of price supports raises the value of the marginal product of workers and, if they get to buy their Grain at subsidized prices, they are better off.)

In India, the landed farmers are not the poorest class; the poorest people are the landless workers. Whether the state of the technology in agriculture is primitive or advanced, technical progress in that sector unambiguously makes workers better off. This is the most important message of this chapter. Its importance, however, will be appreciated better after reading the following chapter, where we shall see that the same cannot be said of the effects of technical progress in industry.

Let us now turn to the empirical picture of Indian agriculture and briefly see what scope there is for improvement. It is commonly argued that agriculture in India has made great strides in the past three decades. It is argued that, while in the mid-sixties India was still importing a substantial amount of foodgrains, by the late seventies and early eighties imports fell to zero. In fact, in 1985 the government held foodgrain stocks that amounted to about 15% of annual foodgrain production. Thus, it would seem, India has become self-sufficient in food.

Professor Dandekar has given a persuasive demonstration of the incorrectness of the above conclusion. He has estimated that from the period 1954–8 to 1976–83 the per capita foodgrain consumption in India went from 181.8 kilograms a year to 185.2 kilograms a year—a trivial increase over twenty-five years. In 1985, the per capita foodgrain production in India was about 200 kilograms a year. Now in terms of calories, consumption of 185.2 kilograms of foodgrain a year generates only 80% of the recommended norm of 2,300 calories per day. (This percentage goes up from 80% to about 90% if consumption of edible oils, sugar, etc. is included.) But the above calculation presumes that the avail-

able foodgrains are equitably distributed over the entire population. If one takes into account the fact that the distribution of income in India is very inegalitarian, the conclusion is inevitable
that a substantial proportion of the Indian population is under-
nourished.

This raises the question as to why the per capita foodgrain
consumption in India hovers around 185 kilograms a year when
the per capita production is about 200 kilograms a year. Professor
Dandekar's answer is compelling. He argues that the income is
distributed in such an inegalitarian fashion that those who are
still hungry do not have the purchasing power to increase their
foodgrain consumption. (If the foodgrain market was truly competitive, the excess supply would be eliminated by a fall in the
price of foodgrains. But the excess supply persists because the
government intervenes in the market and offers to buy up
foodgrain at a price that exceeds the market-clearing level.)

It is clear that improving the lot of the poorest classes requires
not merely an increase in the supply of foodgrains, but also an
increase in the purchasing power of these classes. In particular,
the productivity of labour in agriculture has to be increased. One
way, which we have been exclusively considering so far, is for
agricultural technology to improve. A dramatic example of this is
the introduction of high-yielding varieties (HYVs) of Grain,
which triggered the Green Revolution in the late sixties. The
salutary effects of this new technology, however, have been felt
much more in Punjab, Haryana, and Western UP than in other
states of India. Even in these privileged areas, however, workers
did not gain as much as they could have. This is because the
Green Revolution there was accompanied by the adoption of
labour-displacing technology, such as the use of tractors. Since
capital was subsidized by the government, rich farmers rational-
ly opted for the use of tractors, which they would not have otherwise done. Thus the technical change spurring the Green
Revolution in India was *de facto* rendered somewhat labour-displacing, although this was not the case elsewhere in the world.

The experiences of Punjab and Haryana related above reveal
how important it is for technical change, if it is to help the poor,
to be such that it increases the demand for labour. In our theoretical model we have explicitly assumed that the technical change

is neutral. However, if the technical change is labour-displacing, workers could be made worse off by being rendered redundant.

There is another factor that impinges on how the benefits of a new technology are distributed across the population. This has to do with how the use of new technologies spreads through the agricultural sector. The adoption of such technologies is greatly facilitated by literacy. Rich farmers are usually the first to adopt them and reap their full benefit, because these are the people who have access to education. The poor and illiterate farmers stay with the traditional technologies for long periods of time, because it takes them longer to familiarize themselves with the workings of the new technology. Also, to the extent that the new technologies are perceived as being more risky, poor farmers would be less willing to adopt them. A crop failure with a new and unfamiliar technology may be devastating to a poor farmer, while it would merely be a temporary and minor setback for a rich one. This inequality in the distribution of wealth in rural India handicaps the poor relative to the rich in two ways with respect to the adoption of new technologies: it renders them less educated, and it renders them less able to shoulder risks. As a consequence, one effect of the introduction of a new technology might very well be an even greater disparity between the incomes of the poor and the rich. Agricultural research and extension services set up by the government to help poor farmers adopt new technologies mitigates this problem to some extent. Universal literacy would also greatly help.

There are other ways in which the productivity of labour can be increased in agriculture. Recall that the marginal product of labour increases when higher amounts of other collaborative inputs are used. Two such inputs which are very important are water and fertilizer. (We did not include these in our theoretical framework in order to keep our model simple.) There is considerable scope in India to increase the use of water. In the case of surface water this requires irrigation, and in the case of groundwater it requires pump sets and tubewells. Both these avenues will reduce or eliminate the dependence on rainfall, and so facilitate the taking of more crops each year. By increasing the demand for labour in currently-slack seasons, this would raise the incomes of landless workers, in particular. As of now, only about one-third of the cropped area in India is irrigated, on average. There is considerable potential for increasing the area under irrigation. In some of the poorest states, like Bihar and Madhya Pradesh, more than 50 per cent of the irrigation potential is yet to be exploited.

In the use of fertilizers, India lags behind many developing countries, even behind countries like Indonesia, Pakistan, and Sri Lanka (in terms of amount used per hectare). In 1981, the average amount of fertilizer applied (in kilograms per hectare) was 34 in India, 53 in Pakistan, 74 in Indonesia, 77 in Sri Lanka, 351 in South Korea, and 287 in Taiwan. The use of fertilizers is linked to the availability of water, since the latter crucially affects the productivity of fertilizers. Farmers who have to rely on rainfall which might fail would be less willing to incur the expense of fertilizers than those who have an assured supply of water from irrigation or from tubewells. This reinforces the case for increasing the area brought under irrigation.

The government in India devotes considerable resources to the agricultural sector, but not necessarily in the most efficient manner. For example, farmers are given subsidies for fertilizer, power, and credit. First of all, it is not clear what part of these subsidies accrues to farmers as opposed to the members of the organized sector supplying these inputs to farmers. Moreover, even if these subsidies help raise the incomes of farmers, they work poorly as incentives for encouraging productivity-improving investments. Expenditures devoted to irrigation, on the other hand, would increase this sector's productive potential: given amounts of land and labour can produce more output on irrigated land. It is for this reason that expenditures devoted by the government to increasing the cultivated area brought under irrigation is more in the long-term interests of the Indian economy than expenditures devoted to agricultural subsidies.

There are many ways of improving productivity in agriculture. Irrigation is just one, but an important one. Another avenue, equally important, is agricultural research devoted to improving yields, making crops disease-resistant, etc. In our arguments above, irrigation must be construed as a proxy for various productivity-enhancing activities. Most of these activities share one attribute in common: there is little private incentive for farmers to undertake them, so public investment by the government is warranted. For example, the nature of irrigation is such that, apart from the substantial expenditure involved, its benefits are spread over a large number of people. So no single individual would want to finance such a project, even though it is in the collective interest of all farmers in an area to see the project undertaken. Likewise, no single farmer has the incentive to finance the research expenditure needed to come up with a new variety of superior seeds. This is because once a farmer discovers such seeds, other farmers would find ready access to the new technology by just securing a handful of the new seeds from the innovator's fields. Thus the government can play an important and indispensable role in improving productivity in agriculture.

In the above discussion, we have emphasized the importance of public investment in raising agricultural productivity. Yet, it is the farmer who is the architect of technological change in agriculture. It is he who chooses the technology and decides on the crop-mix. Given proper incentives, there is a great deal of scope for productivity improvements through private investments. For example, the farmer can undertake water-saving over the soil surface. Indian farmers, however, have always laboured under controls which have restricted their freedom to exploit profitable opportunities at home and abroad. For example, although one of the best qualities of cotton is produced in India, there exist controls on cotton exports which adversely affect the incentives of cotton farmers. Such unwarranted controls are a major hindrance to productivity improvements in Indian agriculture.

The rice yield per hectare in India was about 1,750 kilograms in 1990. China and Indonesia's was almost twice this, while South Korea's was much more than twice this. There is thus an enormous gap between yields achieved in India and those achieved elsewhere. This fact, together with the considerable scope for increased use of water and fertilizers in India, suggests that Indian agricultural performance is nowhere near its potential. This offers considerable hope in the future for the 65 per cent of the Indian population that still relies on agriculture for its livelihood.

5

Why Industrial Progress May Not Alleviate Poverty

In this chapter we demonstrate why industrial progress in a less developed country which is closed to international trade may not make the poor better off. In fact, we will show that, under very reasonable conditions, the members of one class can keep benefiting from continued industrial progress, while minimal benefits trickle down to the poorest class, namely, landless workers. So a reliance on industry to deliver the fruits of economic development to the poor may be doomed to fail. In this respect, this outcome is in sharp contrast with our demonstration in the last chapter that agricultural productivity increases invariably benefit the landless workers.

It has been taken as almost a self-evident fact by many people that industrialization and industrial progress are the key to economic growth and poverty alleviation. These, indeed, can be the cornerstones of the desirable kind of economic development that incorporates the poorest classes, but for that to happen certain conditions must be satisfied. If these conditions are not met—as they are not in India—there are certain fundamental forces that will prevent industrial progress from making a dent on poverty. But before we go into a discussion of this, it is necessary to understand the theoretical reasons why the received wisdom in development economics elevates industry to a premier status in the development process. Casual observation is enough to reveal that countries with the highest standards of living are also highly industrialized. But the process by which industrialization causes growth was provided in a classic model by Sir Arthur Lewis. So compelling is the Lewis model as a description of the process of economic development, and so aptly does it fit the economic histories of many of the highly developed countries, that it is imperative for us to digress here and examine the essence of this model.

The Lewis model considers a less developed economy with two sectors: agriculture and industry. The agricultural sector uses two inputs: land and labour. The industrial sector also uses two inputs: labour and capital (i.e. machines). There are two classes of economic agents in the economy: workers and capitalists. The workers earn only wage income and are at subsistence. The capitalists are the industrialists who use their savings to make machines, which are used in conjunction with labour to produce industrial goods. They receive the profits from their operations as payment or compensation for the savings they provide to make machines. Lewis assumes that the capitalists are the savers in the economy; they restrict their own consumption to a minimum and all profits in excess of this they invest in order to make more machines, i.e. to accumulate capital. So industrial workers will have more capital available to them next year as compared to this year, even more the year after, and so on. This is a description of the essential features of the Lewis model as it pertains to the process of economic development.

We must mention, as an aside, that Lewis introduced one concept which has subsequently received a lot of attention and has become a part of traditional thinking. This is the notion of 'surplus labour'. By this concept Lewis attempted to capture the idea that in the agricultural sector of some LDCs like India, labour is so abundant that the marginal product of labour may be zero (or close to it). Clearly, then, wages in that sector could not be determined competitively, for if they were, wages would be zero—which is patently absurd. Lewis proposed a mechanism, alternative to competitive labour markets, which might approximate the way in which wages are determined in the agricultural sector. From the point of view of the essential implication of the Lewis model for the process of economic development—which, as we shall see below, is the transfer of labour from agriculture to industry—the concept of surplus labour is redundant. In other words, the same conclusions emerge whether or not there is surplus labour. So we do not emphasize it here. We shall take it that wages are determined com-

petitively even in agriculture, and if labour is very abundant
these wages will be relatively low.

We can now analyse what effect the accumulation of capital in
industry will have on the well-being of workers. The marginal
product of a worker in industry will depend on the amount of
capital (i.e. the number and sophistication of machines) he has to
work with. A worker with access to a lathe will clearly be more
productive than one who has only a handtool to work with. To
an industrialist, a worker is clearly worth more in the former
case than in the latter, and so would be willing to offer higher
wages in the former case. Suppose in the current year there is a
certain amount of capital available to industry, and the wages offered in industry are exactly equal to that in agriculture. In this
equilibrium there will be a certain allocation of the economy's
labour between industry and agriculture. Next year the amount
of capital available to industry will be higher because the
capitalists would have saved the bulk of their profit so as to
make more machines available to workers. Thus the marginal
product of the existing number of workers in industry will be
higher than before and so the capitalists would want to hire more
workers. But in order to do this, the wages offered to industrial
workers will have to be higher. This will attract some workers
from agriculture and, because fewer workers are left behind to
work the same amount of land, the marginal product of the
remaining agricultural workers will rise. This will bid up the
wages in agriculture. In the new equilibrium of next year, wages
will again be equalized between the two sectors but at a higher
level than this year.

We see from the above discussion that capital accumulation in
industry, by raising the worth of labour in industry, bids up the
wages of workers in both sectors. So workers unambiguously become better off. Also, the process that equalizes wages in the two
sectors brings about a transfer of labour from agriculture to industry. As capital accumulation proceeds year after year, the
well-being of workers secularly improves and more and more of
the labour force is employed in industry. Finally, only an insignificant proportion of the labour force is employed in agriculture.
This is the essence of the Lewis model with regard to the transformation of a less developed economy into a developed one.
This model also provides the theoretical rationale for the convic-

tion, now entrenched, that it is the industrial sector, together with capital accumulation, that spearheads the development process in a closed economy.

The message of the Lewis model to less developed countries was that they should accumulate capital more rapidly, i.e. build more machines, turbines, factories, dams, etc. But people do not consume capital; they consume the goods that capital can help produce in the future. To accumulate capital (in the absence of foreign borrowing), people should be willing to forego consumption now in order that the resources thus saved can be used to build machines. Thus the proportion of a nation's income that is saved, called the *savings rate*, is an indicator of the rate at which the country is accumulating capital. Lewis prescribed that the process of economic development of a less-developed country can be greatly facilitated if the savings rate is increased from about 5 per cent to about 10–12 per cent. India and many other developing countries have achieved savings rates far in excess of this. Yet poverty is rampant; the accumulation of capital has not greatly benefited the poor. Why? What is sabotaging the Lewis process? It is to answer these questions that we now turn.

We first note that one can offer several explanations as to why the Lewis process has not worked in India, which undoubtedly have some validity but which are not fundamental. In other words, even if the phenomena driving these explanations are eliminated, the process of absorption of labour by industry from agriculture would remain stifled. One such explanation might be that technology in industry is progressing but is more and more biased towards capital and, in fact, may tend towards eliminating the use of workers. It is certainly true that technology in Indian industry is becoming more intensive in its use of capital and more labour-displacing in character. Another explanation, which also has an element of truth in it, is that the industrial sector in India is highly unionized, and these unions are preventing the absorption of labour by keeping industrial wages at artificially high levels. Yet another explanation, also with some validity, might be that the Indian economy is over-regulated, and so the economic forces that would normally operate to bring about the reallocation of labour are being impeded. All these explanations, however, are not fundamental. There is something intrinsic in the situation of a closed, underdeveloped economy that could prevent the Lewis process from being worked out even if all the impediments mentioned above (and, possibly, others not mentioned) were eliminated.

Since capital accumulation does not appear to be the key to eliminating poverty in developing countries, we abstract from capital altogether in this chapter and assume, as before, that industry uses only labour. We give to technical progress in industry the central role that capital accumulation played in Lewis' model. This has two advantages. Firstly, the outcome we are about to demonstrate below can also be demonstrated if, as Lewis, we include capital as an input in (only) industry and assume that capital accumulates over time. Since, in other words, capital as an input is irrelevant to the conclusions we deduce below, it is reasonable to abstract from it altogether and keep the model simple. Secondly, the situation of present-day developing countries is somewhat different from that of the developed countries at their corresponding stages of development. The latter had to indigenously develop their technologies; today's LDCs can easily borrow foreign technology at very little cost. Thus rapid technological progress in industry is a realistic characterization of the industrial sectors of present-day LDCs.

Let us now reconsider the two-sector model we introduced in Chapter 3. In the last chapter we held industrial productivity fixed and examined the consequences on the worker and landlord classes of increases in agricultural productivity. Now we reverse the exercise; we hold agricultural productivity fixed and examine how, starting from an initial equilibrium, increases in industrial productivity will affect the two classes. What shall we assume about the initial equilibrium? We saw in the last chapter that, depending on the productivity of agriculture, the equilibrium could be one in which neither class consumes Textiles, only the landlord class consumes Textiles, or both classes consume Textiles. For a country like India, the most realistic situation to assume as the starting point of our analysis is the one in which only the landlords consume Textiles.

Let us, then, assume that the agricultural productivity in India is fixed at a level which, in equilibrium, leaves workers unsated with Grain, but landlords are sated and so are consuming Textiles. Because the economy is in equilibrium, the allocation of labour across the two sectors is such that the total quantities of

Grain and Textiles demanded equal the respective quantities supplied. Starting from this situation, suppose there is a small increase in industrial productivity. By this we mean that less labour (fewer man-hours) is now required to produce one unit of Textiles. What effect will this productivity increase have on the allocation of labour across the two sectors and on the well-being of the two classes?

Since less labour is required to produce a metre of Textiles, the cost of producing a metre declines. Competition amongst textile producers will lower the price of Textiles. Thus those who consume Textiles, namely, landlords, are going to be better off because they can now buy more Textiles with a given income. On the other hand, since workers are not sated with Grain, they will still not buy any Textiles—despite the fact that, relative to Grain, Textiles are now cheaper than before. We saw in Chapter 3 that when tastes are hierarchical, people do not substitute Grain for Textiles and vice versa when the price of one falls relative to the other.

In the last chapter we saw that an increase in agricultural productivity reallocated labour in a manner that increased the value of the marginal product of labour. When industrial productivity increases, however, there is no reallocation of labour. To see this we only need note that following the productivity increase in industry, the landlords demand the same amount of Grain as before because they are sated, while the workers will not demand any less Grain because they will not switch expenditure away from Grain to Textiles. If the total demand for Grain remains the same, so must the total supply, in equilibrium. This, in turn, means that the same number of workers must be employed in agriculture as before, since agricultural productivity in this exercise is constant. It is this fact—that industrial productivity increases do not reallocate labour from agriculture to industry—that is responsible for the agricultural wages (given by the value of the marginal product of labour in agriculture) being insensitive to industrial progress. Since the wage rate in agriculture is constant, so must the wage rate in industry, for the two must be equal if labour does not move from one sector to the other. How can the value of the marginal product of labour in industry be the same as before when the assumed technical progress in industry increases the marginal product of labour?

This occurs because the productivity increase makes Textiles cheaper—in precisely the proportion that the marginal product of labour in industry increases. Since the decline in the price of Textiles precisely offsets the increase in productivity, the value of the marginal product of labour, and hence the wage rate, in industry stays the same as before.

The upshot of all this is that, if initially landlords are sated with Grain and are consuming Textiles while workers are not, an increase in industrial productivity makes landlords better off but leaves workers no better (or worse) off. Furthermore, the allocation of labour across the two sectors remains unchanged. The benefits of the productivity growth, therefore, do not filter down to the poor. Poverty is impervious to industrial progress.

The conclusion drawn above is a powerful one. But at first blush it is possible to think that this is self-evident. After all, one might argue, if workers do not consume any Textiles at all, it is not surprising that they do not benefit from a fall in the price of Textiles. What is so startling about that? To argue in this fashion is to fall into the trap of not thinking in general equilibrium terms. We must realize that, in general it is not necessary to consume a good in order to benefit from a fall in its price. A productivity increase may, and usually does, bring about a reallocation of resources. This reallocation could increase workers' incomes, so that they can buy more of the goods they do consume. In the present case, we would have expected the income of workers to have increased because the productivity of labour in industry has increased. Had this happened, they would have been better off because they could have used the higher incomes to buy more Grain. But this does not happen.

What is essentially responsible for preventing the benefits of industrial progress from filtering down to workers? It is tastes—hierarchical tastes, as determined by the biological need for survival, which dictate that hungry people are not willing to settle for less food in exchange for Textiles (i.e. less agricultural goods for more industrial goods). The fact that the amount of Grain demanded is insensitive to the price of Textiles implies that, in equilibrium, the quantity of Grain supplied should also be insensitive to the price of Textiles. This, in turn, fixes the number of workers required by agriculture. When there is no reallocation of labour, the wage rate remains unchanged.

To see that it is the absence of substitutability between goods in the tastes of consumers that plays the crucial role in generating the above outcome, let us temporarily alter the tastes a bit for the sake of argument. Suppose the tastes were such that at low levels of Grain consumption people are not willing to substitute Textiles for Grain, but at high levels of Grain consumption they might be. Then, following the price decrease of Textiles, landlords would curtail their demand for Grain a bit and increase their demand for Textiles; workers, however, would not. The increase in demand for Textiles and a decrease in demand for Grain would induce a transfer of labour from agriculture to industry, raising the marginal product of labour in agriculture. The wages of workers would be higher and so they could consume more Grain. In this instance, workers would be better off as a result of the productivity increase in industry even though they do not consume any Textiles.

Thus, if the poor are not consuming industrial goods, the extent to which industrial progress benefits them depends on the extent to which the rich are willing to trade-off food for industrial goods. The assumption that there is no substitutability, whatsoever, between the two goods is a rather stark one which greatly simplifies the analysis. In reality, there will be some amount of substitutability between the two goods. But how much? In Chapter 2 we saw that the empirical evidence on this suggests that it is small. Commensurately, the poor who do not consume industrial goods will benefit from industrial progress, but the benefits will be *minimal*.

In the discussion above we have all along been considering the case where workers are not sated with Grain. Let us revert back to our assumption of strictly hierarchical tastes and consider what happens when, in the initial equilibrium, both workers and landlords are sated with Grain. We know from the previous chapter that this is an outcome that is possible only when agricultural productivity is sufficiently high, as is the case in reasonably developed countries. As before, an increase in the productivity in industry will lower the price of Textiles and thus, in the new equilibrium, consumers of Textiles will be better off. There will be no reallocation of labour, however, because the total demand for Grain remains unchanged. The value of the marginal product of labour, and hence the wages of workers, remains unchanged. But the fall in the price of Textiles has increased the purchasing power of a given wage income. Thus, in this instance, workers benefit from industrial progress.

The above outcome demonstrates that if industrial productivity increases are to benefit the poorest class in an economy, the productivity in *agriculture* must be sufficiently high. This is the reason why we argue that agricultural development ought to take precedence over industrial development in the early stages of a country's economic growth. If the agricultural sector is primitive, the fruits of industrial progress accrue largely only to the rich. When the agricultural sector is reasonably advanced, all classes can participate in growth spurred by industrial progress; the benefits of growth are more equitably distributed.

South Korea and Taiwan stand out as examples of countries in which economic growth has been relatively equitable. One reason for this is that both countries have had land reforms which redistributed their land in a relatively egalitarian fashion. This meant that the bulk of the population consumed adequate amounts of food and were willing to spend on industrial goods. Thus industrial progress benefited most people. This shows how important it is to have an egalitarian distribution of land. An egalitarian distribution of wealth generates an egalitarian distribution of income; this is not surprising. But more to the point here, an egalitarian distribution of wealth ensures that all people can partake of the gains from economic growth.

It must be noted here that for land reform to enable the poor to benefit from industrial progress, the land-to-labour ratio must be sufficiently high. If this is not so, an egalitarian land reform would push the entire population below the level at which they are sated with Grain. In this case, a demand for industrial goods would not manifest and there would be no industrial sector in the economy. If we observe the existence of an industrial sector in a densely populated poor country, it is precisely because the distribution of wealth is inegalitarian.

Over the past dozen years or so, agricultural productivity in China has increased at a staggering rate. This has been triggered by the liberalization of the agricultural sector. Among other things, peasants in the countryside are now allowed to sell part of their produce in local markets. The unleashing of self-interest brought about by this break from exclusive communal farming is responsible for a considerable increase in the wealth of the agricultural populace. As a result, if liberalization in industry brings about a similar productivity increase in that sector, the countryside is poised to benefit from it. In fact, the growing wealth of the people in the agricultural sector will likely give a strong fillip to China's industry.

In the previous chapter, on comparing the productivity of Indian agriculture with those of other south Asian countries, we saw that the Indian performance is wanting. We argue, on the basis of our analysis above, that the low productivity characterizing much of Indian agriculture is the major reason why the poor are being left out of the development process in India.

Our arguments regarding the precedence agriculture ought to be given over industry in the early stage of development should not be interpreted to mean that we think industry is unimportant. Our point is that what is important at one stage of an economy's development need not be important at all stages. Indeed, in the later stages of development, industrial progress is crucial. Moreover, industry also produces inputs used in agriculture. Thus a technical change in the industrial sectors producing these inputs will directly impinge on agricultural productivity. The model we have discussed here ignores this link. Technical progress in such industries (e.g. fertilizers) should really be construed as technical progress in agriculture in the context of our model.

In terms of the scope industry offers a country to increase its total income, it has two distinct advantages over agriculture. One advantage operates from the supply side and the other from the demand side. On the supply side, agriculture suffers from diminishing returns to labour because land is a fixed input, while industry does not. So when industry absorbs more labour, wages can be constant, while if agriculture absorbs more labour, wages must fall. Even if industry uses capital and is constrained because there is only so much capital available this year, in subsequent years capital can be increased through savings. In agriculture, the productivity of land can be effectively increased by technical progress, but there are limits to this. On the demand side, agriculture has the disadvantage that beyond a point there is little or no increase in the food demanded as the country's income increases, while there is no such problem facing industry.

Thus there are limits to how rich an agricultural economy can get.

In view of the distinct advantages industry has to offer, it would be foolish to undermine the importance of the sector. Our point, rather, is that for industry to realize its full potential in contributing to equitable growth, agriculture must be well developed.

6

The Economic Consequences of the Luxury Sector

In most developing countries, there is a luxury sector which caters to the demands of the rich. India is no exception. Indeed, the astounding rate at which new luxury goods are being introduced in the midst of poverty betrays the extent to which the development process is benefiting only some privileged classes of the Indian economy. In this chapter, we modify our model by explicitly incorporating an industrial luxury goods sector in order to examine how it affects resource allocation in a closed economy. We will demonstrate that, in the presence of a luxury sector, industrial productivity increases may even harm workers—thereby reinforcing the arguments of the last chapter.

In this chapter we also explicitly introduce capital as an input into the production process. This rectifies one unrealistic aspect of the model used so far, and by doing so we demonstrate that no essential damage was done by neglecting capital in our earlier chapters. But apart from this, explicit consideration of capital introduces another class of agents in addition to landlords and workers, namely, capitalists (the owners of capital). This enables us to get some interesting insights into how class interests in such an economy are aligned. For example, it enables us to inquire if the interests of the landlords are necessarily opposed to those of the capitalists.

We also use the modified model introduced in this chapter to inquire about precisely how population growth impinges on the welfare of the poorest class. The model sheds some light on how rapid population growth can contribute to a polarized development path in which the rich grow richer and the poor stay poor. The ramifications introduced in this chapter thus not only increase the realism of our description of the Indian economy, but also enable us to widen the scope of the issues we can consider.

We now modify the model used in the last three chapters. With respect to consumption, we assume that all individuals have hierarchical tastes for *three* goods: Grain and Textiles, as before, and a luxury good which we call Automobiles. But just as Grain and Textiles were typical representatives for a variety of food items and basic industrial goods, respectively, Automobiles stand as a proxy for a variety of luxury goods such as cars, scooters, refrigerators, televisions, video recorders, washing machines, etc. We now introduce satiation with respect to Textiles also; after he consumes some fixed amout of Textiles (say, 10 metres per month), a consumer does not purchase any more Textiles. Any income left over is now spent on luxury goods. There is no satiation with respect to luxury goods. Thus tastes are, again, strictly hierarchical: only after a consumer has consumed enough Grain will he buy Textiles, and only after he has consumed enough Textiles will he spend on Automobiles. An individual whose income is exhausted even before he is sated with Textiles, for example, will not demand any Automobiles. Thus in the list of priorities, food is at the top, luxury goods are at the bottom and basic industrial goods fall in between.

On the production side, we have three sectors in the economy: an agricultural sector and two industrial sectors, one producing necessary industrial goods and another producing luxury goods. We also make the model more realistic by explicitly introducing capital as an input into the production processes of all three sectors. Agriculture now produces Grain using three inputs: land, labour and capital (tractors, for example). These inputs are substitutable in the production of Grain, i.e. if we had a little less land, for example, output can be maintained by substituting a little more labour and capital.

The industrial sectors use two inputs: labour and capital. These are used in fixed proportions in each of the two sectors, i.e. a fixed amount of labour is required to be used with each unit of capital. For example, the operation of a lathe may call for the use of two workers, and adding another worker would not increase output, while cutting back a worker would reduce output. In other words, to produce a given output in an industrial sector, capital and labour must be used in a fixed proportion. In the above example, this fixed proportion is 1 : 2 (i.e. one unit of capi-tal with two workers). This assumption, which we invoke here for simplifying our thinking, actually is quite realistic. It is often the character of industrial technology that it dictates precisely how much labour is required with the use of a machine.

Even if capital and labour are to be used in fixed proportions, this proportion will differ across the two sectors, in general. It may be that in the Automobile sector capital and labour are re-quired to be used in the ratio 1 : 1, while in the Textile sector the ratio may be 1 : 2. In this case, we will refer to the Textile sector as being more *labour-intensive* than the Automobile sector, since the former requires more labour to accompany a unit of capital. Equivalently, we could say that the Automobile sector is more *capital-intensive* than the Textile sector, since the former needs more capital to accompany one unit of labour. Note that the numbers above refer only to the ratios in which the inputs are to be used, not to the absolute amounts of these inputs. It does not follow, for example, that it is more expensive to make a metre of Textiles than it is to produce an Automobile because both need one unit of capital but the former needs two units of labour while the latter needs only one! In reality, one metre of Textiles may need 1/4 unit of capital and 1/2 unit of labour (so the ratio is 1 : 2), while an Automobile may require 5,000 units of capital and 5,000 units of labour (so the ratio is 1 : 1).

While the numbers given above by way of example are ar-bitrary, we shall assume throughout this chapter that the Automobile sector is more capital-intensive than the Textile sec-tor, or, equivalently, that Textiles are more labour-intensive than Automobiles. This seems to be a realistic assumption to make in the context of present-day India. When we consider luxury goods like refrigerators, washing machines, video recorders and the like, it seems clear that these are highly capital-intensive goods. This is certainly so in comparison with the industrial products that can be thought of as necessities, like footwear, kitchenware, bicycles, etc. It might appear that some luxury ser-vices like five-star hotel services or airline services are very labour-intensive. But they would not appear so if we take into account the enormous amounts of capital required to build such hotels or to purchase the aircraft.

In the two-sector model we used in the previous three chapters, there were only two classes of economic agents, landlords and workers. We had assumed then, and continue to assume now, that the fixed amount of land in the economy was evenly distributed amongst a fraction of the population. There are now three classes of economic agents, capitalists, landlords and workers. By capitalists we mean those agents who own the capital in the economy. We shall take it that in any given year there is a fixed amount of capital in the economy, which is evenly distributed over a fraction of the population. For convenience, we shall assume that landlords are not capitalists, and vice versa. While this assumption is not essential, it helps sharpen our analysis. We can then identify landlords' interests with those of agriculture and capitalists' interests largely with those of industry—which is a fairly realistic characterization.

Just as landlords earn, in addition to labour income, a rental income on their land, capitalists, too, will earn, in addition to labour income, a rental income on their capital. It is important to be clear about what exactly this non-labour component of a capitalist's income consists of. In its broadest sense, by capital one means wealth. (Although wealth includes land, we exclude the latter because we have given it its own category.) If it is used in any production process and it is scarce, capital will receive a payment (i.e. a *return*) as compensation for its services, and that return accrues to its owner. In competitive markets, the return to capital is determined as it is for any other input, namely, by the value of its marginal product. Suppose, holding the amounts of all other inputs fixed, an additional piece of machinery that costs Rs 100 is put into use in agriculture. As a result, suppose the agricultural output increases by 2 kilograms of Grain over the year, and the price of Grain is Rs 5 per kilogram. The value of the marginal product of capital is then = Rs 5 x 2 = Rs 10, which the owner of capital will receive as compensation. At the end of the year he will get back Rs 110, in exchange for the Rs 100 he gave at the beginning and the return on his capital (which is usually expressed as a percentage) is 10 per cent. We mention, in passing, that one need not actively monitor the use of his capital to earn a return. An owner of capital may simply choose to put his money into a savings account offering, say, a 10 per cent interest rate; the bank then undertakes the activity of channelling the capital to those who can use it. (People with substantial amounts of money in their savings accounts are capitalists, whether they realize it or not.)

We are now ready to consider the general equilibrium of this economy. Suppose, to begin with, the economy's three resources are arbitrarily allocated across the three sectors. This allocation will determine the outputs of these sectors. The incomes of the various agents, as determined by the values of the marginal products of the inputs they provide, will determine the quantities demanded of the three goods. If these differ from their respective supplies, the economy is not in equilibrium. Prices will adjust and those sectors facing an excess supply will see an exodus of resources, while those facing excess demand will see an inflow. In the general equilibrium, the market will clear in each of the sectors. In this equilibrium, each economic agent will earn a certain income, which will determine how much he gets to consume of each good, i.e. his level of well-being is determined. Of course, all members of the same class will achieve the same level of well-being. Workers, as before, constitute the poorest class.

What are the amounts of the goods being consumed by the members of the three classes, in equilibrium? That will depend on the relative amounts of labour, land and capital there are in the economy, and also on the productivities in the three sectors. Let us consider the case where, in the equilibrium, workers are not sated with Grain, while landlords and capitalists are not only sated with Grain but also with Textiles, and are consuming Automobiles. In other words, the equilibrium is such that those who earn only labour income are still hungry, while those who receive non-labour incomes as well are rich enough that they patronize the luxury sector. This is not an unrealistic description of the Indian economy.

We are now ready to consider how productivity increases in the three sectors will impinge on the well-being of the members of the three classes, particularly the working class. As in the two-sector model of the previous chapters, one can demonstrate that neutral technical change in the production of Grain (the good which is highest in the list in consumers' tastes), will unambiguously make workers better off. We also saw in the previous chapter that when tastes are strictly hierarchical, a productivity increase in Textiles (the good that was there the lowest in the list of consumers' priorities) made only the consumers of Textiles better off, having no effect on workers. In the present model, the good that is lowest in the list of consumer priorities is the Automobile (the luxury good). One can show that neutral technical progress in the Automobile sector makes capitalists and landlords (i.e. the consumers of Automobiles) better off, but has no effect on the well-being of workers. In order to avoid repetition, however, we leave it to the reader to verify the correctness of these two conclusions by mimicking the logic provided in the earlier chapters. What we wish to explicitly examine, however, are the effects on the equilibrium of technical progress in the production of the good that is intermediate in the list of consumer priorities, in the present model, namely Textiles. (In the model of previous chapters there was no such intermediate good.) These effects, as we shall see below, are startling.

Consider how the equilibrium would be affected by a small, neutral increase in the productivity of the textile sector. By neutral technical progress here we mean that given amounts of capital and labour, though still required to be used in the same ratio as before, produce more Textiles than earlier. It now takes proportionately less capital and less labour to produce one metre of Textiles. The price of Textiles will fall, as a consequence, but the buyers of Textiles (capitalists and landlords) will not purchase any more because they are already sated with Textiles. They will be better off, however, because they have to spend less to meet their fixed demand for Textiles. In other words, the purchasing power of their income has increased. Since the quantity demanded of Textiles is fixed, in equilibrium the quantity supplied will have to be, too. So some labour and capital will be released from the now more-productive Textile sector. Where will these resources flow? To wherever there is an increase in their worth.

The income that the landlords and capitalists saved from having to spend less on Textiles will now be spent on Automobiles, because the luxury good is next in the list of consumer priorities. In order to meet the increased demand, the Automobile sector will expand by absorbing some of the resources released by the Textile sector. But since the Automobile sector is more capital-intensive than the Textile sector, the former will absorb all of the released capital (and, in fact, would want more) but not all of the released labour. The redundant labour will be forced to flow into agriculture. Since agriculture is subject to diminishing returns, the ensuing decline in the marginal product of labour will lower the wage rate. But this is not all.

Since workers' incomes have fallen, their demand for Grain (the only good they consume) will fall; the demands for Grain from capitalists and landlords will stay the same, since they are sated with Grain. For equilibrium to be restored, the supply of Grain must fall, too, whereas the inflow of labour into agriculture would tend to increase the Grain output. So some resource must flow out of this sector. Which resource will it be? It will be capital, because the expanding Automobile sector, which is capital-intensive, will attract capital away from agriculture by offering a higher return. The exodus of capital, by leaving each agricultural worker less capital to work with, will lower the marginal product of labour even more; wages will decline even further.

Ultimately, following the increase in productivity in the Textile sector, the economy will settle down at a new equilibrium after all the processes discussed above work themselves out. In this new equilibrium, capitalists and landlords are unambiguously better off because they get to consume the same amount of Grain and Textiles as before, but more Automobiles. Workers are unambiguously *worse off* because they get to purchase less of the only good they consume, Grain. Neutral technical change in one of the industrial sectors has made the poorest class even poorer.

The unpalatable outcome which obtains above shows how important it is to understand the general equilibrium nature of the interactions involved. What is responsible for this outcome? It is the composition of the demand in an economy that is characterized by extreme disparities in income. On the one hand, we have people in extreme poverty, whose productivity and well-being could be improved if they could each work with more land and more capital. On the other hand, we have people with sufficient non-labour income who are only interested in increasing their consumption of luxury goods. When technical progress in the Textile sector effectively puts more purchasing power in the hands of the rich, they only demand more luxury goods. As a result, not all the workers who are displaced from the (labour-intensive) Textile sector are absorbed by the (capital-intensive)

Automobile sector. Not only are some workers forced into agriculture (so that the land-to-labour ratio declines), the luxury sector also siphons off some capital from the agricultural sector (so that capital-to-labour ratio also declines). Workers are doubly worse off.

The mechanism described above is probably one of the reasons Indian industry is not absorbing workers from agriculture at a rapid enough rate. There is a mushrooming demand for luxury goods coming from a small proportion of the Indian population. In 1975–76, for example, the poorest 40 per cent of the Indian population earned only about 16 per cent of the nation's total income, while the richest 5 per cent of the population earned about 22 per cent of the total income. In 1971, in rural India the richest 10 per cent of the landlords owned over 50 per cent of the assets. It is this sort of inequality in the distribution of income and wealth which is responsible for a substantial market demand for luxury goods in the midst of abject poverty. Since the composition of demand is crucial to determining how the fruits of the growth process are distributed, the pattern of inequitable growth is self-perpetuating. Inequality in wealth generates more inequality.

There is a further undesirable feature of an inegalitarian distribution of wealth across the population: the rich derive mutual benefits from each other. So any attempt to rectify the inequality will be foiled. We can see this by examining the interests of capitalists and landlords in the sensitive issue of land reform. By land reform we mean that the available land in the economy is distributed in a more egalitarian fashion, so that some people who are currently landless workers receive land. The existing landlords, of course, will be vehemently opposed to land reform. What is not apparent, however, is that capitalists, too, will be opposed to land reform—despite the fact that we have assumed capitalists own no land. Let us see why this is so.

As before, let us begin with an economy in an equilibrium in which capitalists and landlords are consuming the goods of all three sectors, while workers are consuming only the agricultural good. Now consider a land reform in which a little bit of land is taken away from each of the present landlords and given to some landless workers. As a result, if the economy's land was originally distributed evenly over, say, 10 per cent of the population, it is now evenly distributed over 11 per cent. How will the new equilibrium differ from the old?

Since the former landlords have lost some land-rental income, the demand for Automobiles will fall. Since this income has been transferred to some workers-turned-landlords, the demand for Grain and Textiles will rise. So the Automobile sector will shrink, while the Grain and Textile sectors will expand. Since the Textile sector is more labour-intensive than the Automobile sector, the former will absorb all of the labour released by the latter (and would want more, in fact), but it will not absorb all of the released capital. The redundant capital will flow into agriculture. Since each worker in agriculture has more capital to work with, the marginal product of labour and, hence, the wage rate will rise. The expanding Textile sector, needing more labour than was released by the Automobile sector, will siphon off some labour from agriculture. By increasing the amount of land per worker in agriculture, this will further increase the marginal product of labour and the wage rate of workers.

As a result of the land reform, those workers who have become landlords are obviously better off in the new equilibrium. More compelling and less obvious is the outcome that even workers who are still landless are bettter off than before. This is because the redistribution of land has shifted demand away from the luxury good, in favour of a labour-intensive good. This also works against capitalists, because the Automobile sector is capital-intensive. When this sector shrinks, capital is reallocated to sectors that use capital less intensively, and so the return on capital falls. The decline in the income from capital to capitalists may be partly or wholly offset by the increase in their wage income. If, however, capitalists do not work—which is not unlikely—they will be unambiguously worse off as a result of the land reform. If the production of luxuries is capital-intensive, capitalists would prefer an inegalitarian distribution of land. An inegalitarian distribution of wealth leads to an inegalitarian distribution of income. The latter generates a demand for luxury goods, which enables the capitalists to thrive. The economic interests of capitalists, therefore, will be aligned with those of landlords in resisting land reform.

The model of this chapter is also appropriate for an analysis of the various effects of labour unions in industry. While agricultural workers are not substantially better off today compared to those forty years ago, the same cannot be said of workers in modern industry. (Firms using modern industrial technology constitute the so-called organized sector of the economy and, for all practical purposes, this is also the sector of unionized workers.) In 1981, for example, the income per worker in the organized sector was three and a half times that of a worker in the unorganized sector. Although the organized sector employed only about one-tenth of the economy's labour force, it received one-third of the nation's income.

If the labour market is perfectly competitive, workers with identical skills will earn the same wage everywhere in the economy. But industrial workers earn much more than agricultural workers because labour unions in industry bargain collectively with their employers to artificially bid their wages up to higher-than-competitive levels. In their collective bargaining, unions use weapons such as the threat of strikes, while managements use threats of lock-outs, etc. There are various demands that unions make, but the bargaining outcome invariably entails union workers receiving wages that are higher than those that would prevail in competitive labour markets. Suppose unions are organized on an industry-wide scale, so that all industrial firms had to pay their workers higher wages. What effects would this have on the equilibrium of the economy? There can be several effects, and we discuss two relevant ones below.

In one respect, the consequences of industrial labour unions are similar to those of land reform. When industrial workers get higher wages, the prices of Textiles and Automobiles would go up commensurately because labour is more expensive. Since Textiles now absorb a larger proportion of landlords' and capitalists' incomes, the demand for (capital-intensive) Automobiles will decline. All of the labour released (and more) from the Automobile sector will be absorbed by the (labour-intensive) Textiles industry, which will experience an increase in demand from the now-richer industrial workers. Some of the released capital will be forced to flow into agriculture, increasing the productivity of labour there. The marginal product of labour will further increase because the expanding Textiles sector would siphon off some workers from agriculture. One result of all this is that the return on capital will fall because the demand for a capital-intensive good has declined. More paradoxically, the formation of labour unions in industry would tend to make agricultural workers better off by shifting demand towards a labour-intensive good.

If the effect described above were all, then one could have argued that the formation of industrial labour unions is good for the poor in agriculture. Unfortunately, there is a countervailing effect which could hurt the poor over the long haul. We have assumed that there was only one technology available for producing each product. If there are many technologies (which use capital and labour in different ratios) with which an industrial good can be produced, firms will choose the one which produces the output at least cost. In a country with abundant labour and scarce capital, firms would pick the most labour-intensive technology available for the product. This is because labour will be cheap in such a country and capital will be expensive; firms will economize on the expensive input.

Now if industrial labour unions manage to bid up the wages of industrial workers, firms will no longer find it profitable to employ the most labour-intensive technology available or to invest in labour-intensive sectors. The shift towards more capital-intensive technologies in industry, induced by an artificial scarcity of labour, will reduce the industrial demand for labour. As a consequence, more workers will be left in agriculture, and the higher land-to-labour ratio means a lower wage rate. This will be reinforced by the fact that industry now will absorb some of the capital that would have gone into agriculture. This implies that the formation of industrial labour unions would tend to make agricultural workers poorer than they would have been. The net result of the two opposing effects described above is uncertain. It is possible that agricultural workers are made worse off by the presence of unions in industry.

The discussion presented above can be readily adapted to examine the consequences of non-neutral labour-displacing technological progress. In our analysis of the effects of productivity increases in industry, we assumed that the technical progress was neutral. What happens if, for example, to produce one metre of output the Textiles industry now needs 2 units of capital and 1 unit of labour, whereas it previously needed 2 units of each input? Clearly, the industrial demand for labour would now be lower, and this would shift workers into agriculture. Thus if neutral technical progress in the Textiles sector lowers the wage rate of workers (as we have already seen), labour-displacing technical progress will only worsen their plight. Since industry often imports and adapts technologies developed in the West, where labour is scarce and capital is abundant, much of the technical change in Indian industry is of the labour-displacing variety. Thus labour—already quite abundant in India—is being rendered increasingly redundant in industry. This is precisely the kind of technical progress that is inimical to the well-being of the poor.

One of the more serious problems confronting India is rapid population growth. A rate of growth of 2 per cent a year doubles the Indian population every thirty-five years. What effects does this have on the development process? The model that we have here is well-equipped to demonstrate some consequences of population growth. It is broadly understood, no doubt, that rapid population growth can be detrimental to economic growth. What is often not well understood is that increases in population can be beneficial to some classes. Furthermore, rapid population growth makes it much more likely that a country's development path is one in which the rich grow richer, while the poor perpetually languish in poverty. To see this, let us begin with the economy in the sort of equilibria we have been dealing with all along in this chapter. Then suppose the population of the economy increases slightly, while the amount of land and capital stay the same. To keep the analysis simple, assume the population increase comes essentially from the working class. How is the equilibrium going to be affected?

Since in industry labour is used in fixed proportions with capital, the entire increase in the labour force will be initially forced to flow into agriculture. This will clearly lower the wage rate. But because of the increased labour employed, land and capital in agriculture will experience an increase in their marginal products, and so the land-rental rate and the return on capital will increase. If capitalists and landlords do not work or if their labour income constitutes a negligible proportion of their total income, they will be better off. The demand for Automobiles will increase, as a result. The capital-intensive Automobile sector will expand by absorbing from agriculture some labour but a lot of capital. Workers in agriculture now will be doubly worse off as a consequence. In the new equilibrium, the wage rate will be lower and the luxury sector will be larger than in the old equilibrium.

In essence, what is driving the above phenomenon is the fundamental principle that when the size of the labour force increases, the marginal product of labour goes down, while those of land and capital (the other inputs used in conjunction with labour) go up. Thus an increase in the labour force works to the advantage of economic agents who largely live off non-labour income. Since these are also the people who have only an unsatiated preference for luxury goods, the luxury sector absorbs even more of the scarce capital to meet this demand. Workers are pushed to even lower levels of Grain consumption. A developmental path in which the poorest do not share the benefits of industrial progress is, thus, even more likely.

What can be done in these circumstances to alleviate the abject poverty of the masses? The productivity of labour must somehow be bolstered. If the rate of growth of population cannot be reduced, there are two broad avenues open.

One way is to try and maintain the capital-to-labour ratio in the economy, so that each worker's productivity does not decline on account of having less capital to work with. In fact, to compensate for the decline in the land-to-labour ratio, the capital-to-labour ratio will have to secularly increase. If not, an agricultural worker's productivity would fall. But this requires an increase in the economy's savings rate. For the capital-to-labour ratio to be increased, the total amount of capital in the economy must grow faster than the population. This becomes increasingly infeasible if the latter rate is large; there are limits to the savings potential of people.

Even if the savings rate of the nation can be raised, all is not well. One of the essential aspects of development is an increase in each individual's capital in a very special form: skills and education. Indeed, *human capital* as it is called, can be construed as the most important form of capital in a nation. It is this, more than physical capital (i.e. machinery, equipment etc.), that enables people to expand the scope of their activities, to exercise their ingenuity, to increase their receptiveness to new ideas, and to improve the conditions around them. This requires a substantial investment in a country's educational facilities. All the highly

developed nations, without exception, have a substantial proportion of their wealth in the form of human capital. Literacy rates
(the proportion of the population that can read and write), which
are poor but convenient proxies for human capital, approach 100
per cent in these countries. Now if, due to rapid population
growth, most of a developing country's savings are devoted to
just ensuring that each worker has the requisite physical capital,
little will be left over for investing in human capital. The
country's workforce will largely remain unskilled.

In the important matter of education, India's performance has
been very poor compared to other developing countries. In 1991,
only about 52.2 per cent of the Indian population could read and
write. About 60 per cent of all expenditure on education in India
comes from various levels of government, and the rest comes from
private sources. The field of education is a legitimate area for the
government to play an even bigger role. The returns to expenditure
on education are very high. From society's point of view the
returns are even greater than the (private) returns to an individual's
educational expenditure. Not only does an educated person
produce output of higher value (as reflected by the higher income),
but others are able to learn from him or her and, to some extent, are
able to educate themselves at little or no cost. This is one important
difference between physical capital and human capital. Skills embodied in people can be transferred to others who do not have
those skills. Nothing of the sort is true of physical capital. Another
crucial difference is that human capital is capable of conceiving and
creating newer and more productive forms of physical capital. The
developed countries of today achieved their present standards of
living not merely by accumulating physical capital, but by encouraging continual innovation.

Most developed countries devote well over 5 per cent of the
country's income to education. In developing countries this percentage ought to be higher. In 1979, India spent only about 3.2
per cent of its income on education. Even countries like Egypt
(4.1 per cent), Tanzania (5.75 per cent), and Malaysia (8.5 per
cent) did better in this respect. Furthermore, a disproportionate
amount of the government's educational expenditures in India is
assigned to high school and university education. If this bias
towards higher education is eliminated, fewer people would be
illiterate.

This brings us to the other option that can be followed to help the poor in the face of rapid population growth: devoting resources to bring about technical progress in agriculture.* This, ultimately, is the only way for a closed economy to counter the damage done by the diminishing returns induced by land. We have seen in an earlier chapter the importance of agricultural technical progress in raising workers' living standards. (It was by ignoring the possibility of technical progress in agriculture that Malthus, the nineteenth century English economist, arrived at the gloomy prediction that population growth condemns a country to subsistence—an incorrect prediction that earned economics the unfortunate title of 'dismal science'.) The rapid rate at which the population of India is increasing only reinforces the case for an active government role in raising agricultural productivity.

---

*The causes of high rate of population growth, though extremely interesting, are not discussed in this book. We would like to mention, however, that agricultural productivity growth as well as primary education (especially of women) play a key role in reducing the rate of population growth.

7

Will International Trade Harm the Poor?

Consider a landless agricultural worker living hand to mouth in an Indian village. We have seen already that his poverty is impervious to the industrial progress taking place in the country. It is only the rich Indian consumers who benefit from such industrial progress. It is important to remember, however, that our arguments so far have presupposed a closed economy in which the industrial sector produced only to meet the domestic demand. Would a landless agricultural worker benefit in any way if Indian industry could export its output to the West? At the outset, the question seems ridiculous. It should be irrelevant to a poor worker in Bihar whether it is a rich man in New York or one in Bombay who wears a suit cut from a fabric made by Reliance Industries in Bombay. And yet, among all the developing countries, the only countries to have had a sustained, rapid, and significant increase in the wages of the least-skilled workers have been the export-oriented economies of South Korea, Taiwan and, more recently, Malaysia and Indonesia. It is widely known that such economies grew fast, but it is less widely known that this fast growth has been associated with receding poverty. The question is why. Why is it that the export of industrial goods can help alleviate poverty? This is the question we address in this chapter.

Export-led development is, of course, a controversial subject. On the one hand, it is championed by conservative institutions such as the World Bank and the International Monetary Fund and, on the other hand, it is criticized by the Left as detrimental to the interests of the poor. It is not difficult to understand why someone aware of India's colonial history would be suspicious of a development strategy that emphasizes raising exports to the

West. In the middle of the nineteenth century, as the industrial revolution was gathering steam in Great Britain, Indian exports of raw materials like cotton, indigo, and even foodgrain (all referred to as primary exports) rose dramatically. Yet, there is little evidence to suggest that this had a positive impact on the poor multitudes in India. In fact, there have been claims by Indian historians that this pattern of trade with Great Britain resulted in the de-industrialization of India. Many artisans, especially spinners, could not compete with the products of the industrial revolution and had to join the ranks of the landless agricultural workers.*

Similar arguments have been made in the context of Latin America in the nineteenth century. Many countries in that region experienced a tremendous boom in their primary exports, either agricultural products or mineral deposits, as Europe industrialized. But the available evidence, albeit fragmentary, suggests that the poor languished while landlords got rich throughout Latin America during this period. Some Marxist scholars such as Samir Amin, Emmanuel, and Andre Gunder Frank have argued that trade with the West will always be an unequal exchange, and is more likely to retard development than to aid it. It is clear from their writings that their views have been shaped by their reading of colonial history, and especially by the historical experience of Latin America. An examination of the historical record of colonialized countries does raise an interesting question: if export-led growth can alleviate poverty, why did the primary export booms in India and Latin America fail to do so?

Let us try to answer this question in terms of the theoretical framework we have created in the earlier chapters. For convenience, once again we will think in terms of a simple model that will capture the essential process at work when an under-

*There is a great deal of controversy among historians about whether there was any significant de-industrialization in India resulting from British imports in the nineteenth century. The empiricial methods that the available data permit are highly questionable, and this is why neither side in the controversy can be said to have presented a compelling case. There is a consensus, however, that the poor in India gained little despite a pretty sizeable boom in India's primary exports in the second half of the nineteenth century. Theoretically, it seems likely that there was some de-industrialization and that the land-to-labour ratio decreased in Indian agriculture.

developed country (India) engages in trade with a developed country (England). Suppose each country produces two goods: an industrial good (Textiles) and an agricultural good (Grain). We will assume that people have identical (hierarchical) preferences across the two countries. To keep the arithmetic simple, we take it that the price of Grain is Rs 1 per kilogram. Thus, each individual spends all his income on Grain if his income is below a certain minimum level, say G rupees, and spends G rupees on Grain and the remainder on Textiles if his income exceeds G rupees. As in the earlier chapters, the purpose of assuming hierarchical tastes is to capture the observation that the poor spend almost their entire incomes on food while it is mostly the rich who spend on industrial goods. Although we assume identical tastes across the two countries, we will acknowledge one major difference—workers in England are rich enough (i.e. they have incomes above G rupees) to consume Textiles, while the workers in India are too poor (i.e. they have incomes below G rupees) to do so. Let us suppose that the industrial revolution has already started in England, and its industrial exports have invaded the Indian market. Thus, England is exporting Textiles to India and, to pay for the industrial imports, India is exporting Grain to England.

What would happen to workers in each country if the industrial productivity in England rises further as a consequence of the continuing technical progress there? The cost of production, and hence the price, of English Textiles will decline. Indian consumers would substitute imported Textiles for the domestic product. The price of Textiles in India would drop, because Indian producers will find few buyers at the original price. Indian industry which has not experienced a corresponding productivity increase would face hardship. As the price of Textiles drops, so will the value of the marginal product of labour, and, therefore, the industrial wage. Because the market for the product of Indian industry is shrinking, many textile workers in India would be laid off. These workers, now unemployed, would have no choice but to become agricultural workers. The exodus of workers from industry to agriculture will continue until the land-to-labour ratio has decreased to the point where the wage in agriculture is the same as that in industry. Thus, the poor in India would be made poorer by the industrial progress taking place in

England. Indian workers, who are too poor to buy Textiles, would derive no benefit from the reduced price of Textiles. There would be a greater amount of Grain produced in India due to an increase in the amount of labour engaged in agriculture. But the additional Grain produced would not be available for the consumption of Indian workers; it would be exported to England to pay for the increased imports of English Textiles. Surprisingly, this impoverishment of Indian workers occurs in the midst of a primary export boom in India. If there were no trade with the dynamic economy of England, the poor in India would be shielded from the damaging effects of these events beyond their control. It is not surprising, therefore, that the primary export booms of the nineteenth century in the underdeveloped world did little to alleviate poverty. It is very likely, in fact, that they aggravated it.

The landlords in India, on the other hand, would gain handsomely from India's trade with England. Not only would Textiles, a good they consume, become cheaper to them as a result of industrial progress in England, but their rental income from land would rise as the land-to-labour ratio decreases. In other words, the movement of displaced workers from industry to agriculture would result in more intensive cultivation of land, increasing rents and reducing wages. The process that would make the poor poorer would also make the rich richer.

Trade with England could be rendered advantageous to the poor if land rents were taxed and the resultant revenues were used to subsidize wages. Unfortunately, such a policy, however desirable, has always remained politically infeasible. The distribution of political power has always been related to the distribution of wealth. Typically, the state policy in the underdeveloped societies of primary exporting regions, whether in nineteenth century Bengal or in present-day El Salvadore, has been dominated by landed oligarchies. It is inconceivable that rulers would tax themselves to subsidize the poor. It is easy to understand, then, why free trade with the West was the official policy of so many underdeveloped countries in the nineteenth century and why so many scholars feel that such a policy is detrimental to the interests of the poor.

There is a lesson in this even for modern-day India. If all industrial sectors of the Indian economy are opened up suddenly to imports from more advanced countries there would be a sudden rise in the ranks of the unemployed within the industrial labour force. Many of these workers are bound to return to their villages looking for employment in agriculture. The consequent decline in the land-to-labour ratio will depress wages. The brunt of sudden trade liberalization will be thus borne by the poor. If India continues to practice free trade with a country (or a set of countries) that is experiencing faster industrial progress, the poor in India will continue to get poorer. As we will see later, whether trade liberalization will benefit a developing country depends upon how it is implemented.

There are, however, countries in which the poor benefited from a policy of exporting primary products to more industrialized countries. Some notable examples are the United States of America, Canada, and Australia. These countries developed by exporting agricultural goods to their mother country, England, which had already undergone an industrial revolution. There are three characteristics that distinguish these countries from countries in Latin America and South Asia for whose workers such a developmental path holds little attraction. First, except for the plantation economy of the Southern United States, agricultural production was carried out on family farms. Typically, there was no sharp division between landlords and workers: a worker was a family member who, as a co-owner, shared the rental income. An increase in land rents resulting from a primary export boom compensated—in fact, more than compensated—for the accompanying decrease in wages, if any. Second, these were all land-abundant countries; it was labour that was scarce. There were huge tracts of land waiting to be brought under cultivation. If the demand for wheat and hence its price increased as a result of growing prosperity in England, it then became profitable to bring more land under cultivation. In contrast to what happened in India and Latin America, where the same amount of land got cultivated more intensively in response to the developments in England, the total amount of land employed in agricultural production increased along with labour in these countries. There was little reduction in the land-to-labour ratio and hence in wages. Third, an average farmer in these countries operated enough land to command an income high enough to be able to consume industrial goods. The availability of cheaper industrial goods, therefore, was definitely to his benefit. A historian's view on the desirability of development led by primary exports would thus depend upon the region that is the focus of his or her study.

Let us come back to our model of trade between India and England and ask how the workers in England are affected by industrial progress in their own country. Even if there were no trade with another country, they would benefit from a fall in the price of Textiles since they are consumers of industrial goods. But the trading relationship with India, a supplier of primary goods, further enhances the benefits they derive from the progress in their industrial sector. Not only does the ability to make cheaper Textiles increase the quantity of Textiles demanded at home, but it enables England to capture a bigger market in India. If the labour allocation between the two sectors remained unchanged, the entire increase in the Textile production resulting from the productivity increase would be absorbed domestically as it was in the absence of trade—a case we analysed in an earlier chapter. In order to satisfy the additional demand for Textiles coming from India, more English labour would be employed in industry. Interestingly, such a reallocation of labour can be accomplished without there being a shortfall in supplies of Grain demanded by the population in England, because the ability to export more Textiles translates into the ability to import more Grain. As labour is moved from agriculture to industry, the land-to-labour ratio increases and the wage of English workers rises. Trade with India can thus make the English workers better off at the *expense* of the workers in India. The trading relationship between the two countries has thus very different consequences for the working classes of the two countries. This asymmetry in the gains from trade is the main reason why trade with industrialized countries is an anathema to left-wing intellectuals in the Third World.

What is the main source of asymmetry between England and India in the analysis above? It is that industrial productivity is growing in England and not in India; it is not that England is at a higher level of industrialization. The fact the England is more industrialized than India would cause a quantum decline in the living standards of the poor in India at the time the trading relationship is initiated. But this would be a single blow. A more unfortunate fate for India'a poor would be a continuous decline in their standard of living. From the analysis presented in the previous paragraph, it can be seen that such a fate would result from trading with a country whose industrial progress is faster than India's. Whether wages increase or decrease in India depends upon whether the land-to-labour ratio in India increases or decreases. This, in turn, depends upon whether labour moves from agriculture to industry or vice versa. If productivity in Indian industry were to rise at a faster rate than in British industry, labour in India would move from agriculture to industry. This would be true even if England, being more industrialized, had an advantage in producing and hence exporting industrial goods. Suppose that initially India was importing Textiles from England. As the rate of growth in its industiral productivity begins to outpace that in England, her own industrial sector begins to expand at the expense of England's, causing a reallocation of Indian labour from agriculture to industry. At some point in time, the advantage in producing industrial goods shifts to india thus reversing the pattern of trade between the two countries. Contrast this with what would have happened if there existed no trading relationship with England. As we saw in an earlier chapter, in the absence of international trade an increase in industrial productivity in India would have made industrial goods cheaper to the rich without bringing about any reallocation of labour; Indian wages would be unaffected by its industrial progress. The driving force behind an improvement in living standards of the working class is productivity growth; international trade works as an essential catalyst.

However, is it realistic to expect that an underdeveloped country could outpace a developed country in its industrial productivity growth? The answer is a resounding yes. First, we will examine the theoretical reasons and then the historical evidence.

The task of increasing industrial productivity is qualitatively different for a late industrializing country than it was for the early developers. For the former, the task is to adapt the available technological knowledge to their own needs and environment, whereas for the latter, the task is to invent new knowledge. Although adapting technology to a substantially different environment is not an easy task, it is by no means as difficult as pushing the technological frontier further out. Learning an existing technique is clearly easier than inventing one. This is especially true in the context of industrial technology. In agriculture, a technology tends to be specific to the climate and the soil. In industry, it is much more transferable. In fact, there is great fear in the developed countries that unless they innovate faster they would lose markets to the newly industrializing countries that are gaining on them. It is inevitable that the industries in which there is little innovation would be jettisoned by the developed countries and be picked up by those at their heels.

Before England had an industrial revolution it was India, in fact, that exported Textiles to England and not the other way around. As industrial productivity grew in England, the pattern of trade reversed, since Indian productivity remained stagnant. What England could do then, India can do now. In fact, this is what Japan has accomplished. In the early part of the twentieth century, the productivity growth in Japanese textile mills raced past that in the mills of their Indian and British competitors, capturing markets at home and abroad, and in the process moving labour from agriculture to industry. In the sixties Taiwan and in the seventies South Korea emulated the Japanese example. According to the World Bank Development Report (1990), during the last two decades the average labour productivity (output per worker) in South Korean industry grew at roughly twice its average rate in the highly developed countries comprising the OECD (Organization of Economic Cooperation and Development). Consequently, the proportion of the labour employed in South Korean agriculture fell from 77 per cent to 20 per cent during the period 1950–88; industrial progress in South Korea has certainly made a dent in the living standards of her poor. Fig. 7.1 offers a comparison of the performances of South Korea and India.

It can indeed be tiresome to see South Korea held up as an example to be emulated by other developing countries. South Korea, it is said, is unique. Its authoritarian political structure allows it to pass draconian labour laws that would be unthinkable in India. Its small size and relatively homogeneous population allows its government to focus its energies on the crucial task of productivity growth. But suppression of organized labour is neither necessary nor desirable for bringing about productivity growth. And a large size, in fact, can be an advantage rather than a disadvantage since modern manufacturing technology requires

Why Poverty Persists in India

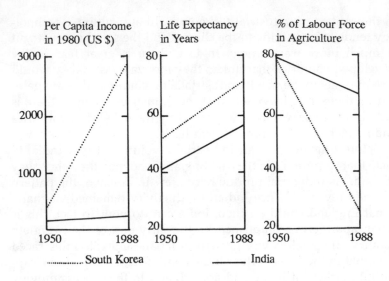

Source: *The Economist,* 23 Sept. 1989.

FIG. 7.1   *South Korea and India: A Comparison.*

production on a large scale to keep the average costs down.
Governing the heterogeneous multitudes in India is indeed a
daunting task, and yet, despite all odds, India has made great
strides is acquiring technological know-how and creating a
labour force with the requisite skills. It is difficult to sustain the
argument that cultural and social factors would inhibit India
from outcompeting Western industry in at least some sectors.

Sometimes it is argued that Taiwan and South Korea adopted
their export-led growth strategies during a particularly
favourable period. The decade of the sixties saw a boom in the
West and there was little resistance to accepting imports from
developing countries at that time. The political climate is different now. The successful performances of Japan and her
emulators in the Far East have shaken the confidence of
businessmen in the West. First in textiles, then in automobiles
and consumer electronics, Asian industries have expanded at the
expense of their counterparts in the West. Real wages have fallen
in North America over the last eighteen years, while they have

risen in Japan, South Korea, and Taiwan. The fear of trading with rapidly industrializing economies is no longer restricted to scholars and policy-makers in the Third World. Consequently, there is much greater pressure today on Western governments to restrict competition from the industrial sectors of developing countries. India can hardly hope to replicate today the successful drive of South Korea during the sixties and seventies.

However, the above arguments merely point out that the task before India today is a lot harder than what South Korea had to face at its comparable stage of development. They do not say that India will not be able to find export markets abroad. Despite all the political resistance mounted by industrial lobbies and trade unions in the West, industrial exports from developing countries to the West have continued to increase. In fact, it is the agricultural sector in the West that may be more difficult to penetrate. The impasse in the latest Uruguay round of GATT negotiations was over the reluctance of members of the European Common Market to open up their countries to trade in agricultural commodities. Food is of strategic importance in the minds of policy makers. The thought of the bankruptcy of domestic food producers, resulting from lowering trade barriers, may account for their intransigence in this matter. Under no circumstances are they willing to depend totally on other countries for the most essential of commodities. The political economy of the creation of trade barriers to industrial imports is not so simple. Allowing cheaper fabrics from India into the US may be opposed by textile manufacturers but would be welcomed by garment manufacturers as well as by consumer lobbies in America. Despite the tremendous opposition by American labour unions fearful of competition from the cheap Mexican labour, a free-trade pact between the two countries is well on its way to being signed.

Protective measures can stem the tide of cheaper imports into Western markets for a short time but certainly not for ever. Witness India's own performance over the last two years: its industrial exports grew by 12.8 per cent per annum from 1985 to 1988. Indonesia, Malaysia, and Thailand are presently in the throes of their own industrial revolutions fuelled by industrial exports. There are tell-tale signs in the department stores of North America: increasingly, the merchandise displayed, especially clothes and toys, are made in these Asian countries. Even

China, a socialist country, seems to place a great deal of premium on being able to sell its industrial goods in Western markets. Despite the disapproval and even condemnation of its repressive policies by the Western governments in the aftermath of Tiananmen Square, China has expended a lot of political capital to maintain the status of a 'most favoured trading nation' that it had won from the US government. There is little reason, therefore, to believe that India, or any other developing country for that matter, faces an impossible task in being able to find markets for its industrial products.

Should we conclude from the above analysis simply that trade is beneficial to the poor in a developing country if it exports industrial goods and harmful if it exports primary goods? Not yet. When we discussed the failure of India and other primary exporting economies (e.g. Latin America) to alleviate poverty, we did not emphasize the fact that the asymmetry across the trading partners arose, not only from the difference in the types of goods exported (i.e. primary vs. industrial), but also from where the productivity growth responsible for the trade boom was taking place. The primary export boom was merely a result of an increase in demand for primary products caused by rising levels of income in the West which, in turn, were caused by industrial productivity growth there. Many so called primary export booms in history have indeed been caused by increases in foreign demand, rather than by increases in the productivity growth in the primary sector of the primary exporting country. But clearly, it is possible that a primary export boom is caused by a boost in agricultural productivity or a discovery of iron ore deposits or an innovation in mining coal. How beneficial would trade be to the poor in the primary exporting country under such circumstances? Going back to our example of trade between India and England, suppose that this time the impetus to trade comes from an increase in India's agricultural productivity growth. As this would lower the international price of Grain, workers as well as landlords in both countries are likely to benefit from it. This means that neutral technical progress in agriculture would be beneficial to all in this case, as it would be in a closed economy. So far we have treated technical change in agriculture as something completely beyond the control of individual farmers. In reality, it is quite possible that trade and the possibilities of exports can create appropriate incentives for farmers to undertake productivity-improving investments.

Thus, trade can benefit the poor in more than one way. If India is able to increase her industrial productivity at a fast enough rate and become an industrial exporter, labour will be moved from agriculture to industry and real wages will rise. Trade can also induce agricultural productivity growth and make a direct impact on the living standards of the poor. The uneasiness that many intellectuals, especially those on the Left, feel about trading with developed countries stems from the possibility of a trade which is not accompanied by any productivity improvements at home. India, with its substantial infrastructure and one of the largest pools of technical manpower, is well poised to narrow the gap in industrial productivity between the developed countries and itself. And without trade, the gains from industrial progress will be confined to the rich.

8

Trade as an Engine of Growth

Trade has been described by some as an engine of growth because it has helped the incomes of some countries to grow very rapidly. In this chapter, we will show that whether or not trade would work as an engine of growth also depends upon the pattern of trade.

The very first thing we have to settle is what determines the pattern of trade. Does England export Textiles and import Grain, or is it the other way around? If England produces Textiles at a lower cost but Grain at a higher cost than India does, it is clear that England will export Textiles in exchange for Grain. But, would there be trade at all if England were more efficient at producing both? Why should England be interested in buying anything from India when she can produce both goods cheaper at home? The answer, known as *the principle of comparative advantage,* is one of the most interesting propositions in economic theory, and it might be worthwhile to take a moment to understand this very fundamental principle. It clarifies why trade between any two countries is considered potentially beneficial to both of them. It shows that whether a country is exporting Grain or Textiles, it stands to gain from international trade. Our purpose in introducing the principle of comparative advantage at this point is to ensure that the reader will be able to contrast it with our argument and understand our point of departure.

A trading relationship between two individuals is based on exactly the same principle as a trading relationship between two countries, and, for most people, the former might be easier to relate to. We will, therefore, illustrate the principle of comparative advantage by presenting a simple model of such a relationship between two individuals—say, Singh and Jones—rather than be-tween two countries like India and England. Suppose that each individual can work a maximum of eight hours per day and also that labour is the only scarce resource in the economy. In other words, the maximum amount of any good that either Singh or Jones can produce is determined by how many hours of labour per day he devotes to the particular production activity and by nothing else. The fact that any production activity in real life re-quires other inputs such as capital and land is irrelevant to the point we want to make here, and we might as well keep our model simple by assuming that labour is the only input in production. We will assume that there are only two goods, Grain and Textiles, that each of these individuals can produce. The measure of each individual's productivity is the amount of each good the individual can produce with an hour of labour. Sup-pose that in one hour, Jones can produce either two kilograms of Grain or two metres of Textiles while Singh can produce only one kilogram of Grain or one-half metre of Textiles. Notice that Jones is more productive than Singh in both activities, but the dif-ference in their productivities is relatively higher in Textiles, as will be made clear shortly. It is this fact that is going to be crucial in determining the pattern of trade between them.

Let us first consider the situation that prevails before a trading relationship is established between the two individuals. If Jones spends all the time at his disposal (i.e. 8 hours) producing Grain he will produce 16 kilograms of Grain and no Textiles. On the other hand, if he spends all his time producing Textiles he will have 16 metres of Textiles but no Grain. In fact, he can have dif-ferent combinations of Grain and Textiles depending upon how he allocates his time. For example, if he divides his time equally between the two activities he will have 8 units of each good. Clearly, in the absence of trade what Jones can consume is con-fined to the different combinations of Grain and Textiles he can produce, which are determined by the time at his disposal and by his productivity. Depending upon his tastes he will pick any one combination of Grain and Textiles from all these production possibilities. Let us suppose that his tastes dictate that he con-sume 4 kilograms of Grain and 12 metres of Textiles. Jones will, therefore, allocate 2 hours to Grain production and 6 hours to Textiles production.

In the absence of trade, Singh's choice of consumption is also limited to what he can produce, given the time at his disposal and his own productivity. If he spends the entire period of 8 hours producing Grain, he will be able to produce a maximum of 8 kilograms of it and no Textiles; at the other extreme, he will be able to produce 4 metres of Textiles and no Grain. If he divides his time equally between the two activities he will produce 4 kilograms of Grain and 2 metres of Textiles. Like Jones, Singh's allocation of his time across the two production activities will be dictated by his tastes. Let us suppose that he chooses 4 kilograms of Grain and 2 metres of Textiles and, therefore, decides to split his time equally across the two activities.

Now let us see how trade between Jones and Singh can be mutually advantageous to both of them. Under what conditions would Jones be willing to trade? First, consider the situation without any possibility of trade. For every hour of work Jones takes away from Textile production to allocate to Grain production he will have to forego 2 metres of Textiles, but in compensation he will gain 2 kilograms of Grain. The cost of producing an extra kilogram of Grain to Jones is really one metre of Textiles foregone. Economists refer to this as the *opportunity cost* to Jones of producing Grain. If Singh offers Jones Grain at a lower rate than Jones' opportunity cost, say, at a kilogram of Grain for three-fourth metre of Textiles, Jones would be interested in an exchange. For example, instead of spending 2 hours producing Grain and 6 hours producing Textiles, he is better off spending all 8 hours producing Textiles and then exchanging 3 metres of Textiles for 4 kilograms of Grain produced by Singh. Such a trade enables Jones to consume 4 Kilograms of Grain and 13 metres of Textiles while without the trading possibility he would consume only 4 kilograms of Grain and 12 metres of Textiles. If Singh could indeed make him such an offer, Jones would be able to add to his consumption 1 metre of Textiles without sacrificing any Grain, and this despite the fact that he is more efficient than Singh at producing both goods. But, would Singh find it advantageous to make such an offer? The answer is yes. He is better off specializing in the production of the good he is relatively less inefficient in, namely Grain, and then trading it for the other good. Because, in exchange for 4 kilograms of Grain Singh would be able to get 3 metres of Textiles thus allowing him to improve his own consumption by 1 metre of Textiles without sacrificing any Grain. Each individual can thus improve his own consumption by producing more of that good which he is more efficient at producing relative to the other good and then engaging in trade with the other individual. In economics, such relative efficiency in a trading situation is termed *comparative advantage*. In the above example, Jones has a comparative advantage in Textiles while Singh, who though less efficient than Jones also at producing Grain, has a comparative advantage in Grain. Trade, according to comparative advantage, makes both trading partners better off compared to the situation when the consumption of each was confined to what he could produce. Trade is thus *mutually advantageous*.

Nothing of significance changes if, in the above reasoning, we substitute countries for individuals as long as we assess the effect of trade in terms of the goods available for consumption to the residents of each country. This is really the foundation of the conventional wisdom on the desirability of engaging in unrestricted trade for any country, no matter what stage of development it is at. Clearly, the statement that a certain country has comparative advantage in *nothing* or *everything* would only reveal that the person making the statement has not understood the concept of comparative advantage.

In our example, we had assumed that each of the trading parties, Singh and Jones, had 8 hours of labour time at their disposal whether or not they engaged in trade. Despite this, trade enabled them to expand their possibilities for consumption. It is easy to see that these gains from trade would have been even higher if the improved incentives resulting from trade made each individual work harder. Note that the decision to work 8 hours a day could itself be a choice made by an individual based on the compensation (or, rewards) for the time he spends working. If an extra hour of work sufficiently increases the consumption of goods he will be able to buy with the extra money, he might be willing to sacrifice some leisure and work, say, 9 hours rather than 8. But as soon as an individual decides to increase his worktime to 9 hours, his capacity to produce each good increases. The other individual may respond similarly to the improved incentives to work created by the opportunity to trade, thereby further increasing his level of consumption. This beneficial effect of trade working through the expansion of production capacities, is not captured in the conventional argument about the gains from trade associated with the principle of comparative advantage. This is the effect that we want to examine in some detail in this chapter. The conventional argument assumes that the resources (or, factors of production) such as labour, land and capital at the disposal of a party engaging in trade remain unchanged despite the changed incentives faced by their suppliers. We want to analyse trade between a developed country and an underdeveloped country without making such an assumption because we believe that changes in the supplies of inputs can significantly alter the impact of trade.

Over thirty years ago, Hla Myint, an economist at Columbia University, wrote about this additional source of gains from trade. He called the process at work *the vent for surplus*, the idea being that trade opened a vent or an outlet for a resource that had been previously underutilized. This was an apt description of the development driven by agricultural exports in the second half of the nineteenth century that transformed the land-abundant economies of Canada and the United States. As the demand for wheat, beef and dairy products from rapidly industrializing European economies grew, incentives were created for clearing and cultivating land that had been considered too expensive to farm before the boom. This triggered a westward expansion. Railroads were built against all odds, spanning the entire continent from the Atlantic to the Pacific ocean. This great increase in the supply of productive resources—the new land under cultivation, the new capital in the form of a transportation network, and the new labour through increased immigration—could all be attributed to the impetus the economy received through an opportunity to trade. An increase in demand from overseas for a good in which the North American economies had a comparative advantage raised the rewards to human effort at many levels. Homesteaders (aspiring family farmers) agreed to move to remote areas. Rail engineers took unprecedented risks. None of this would have been possible if there had been no anticipation of increased opportunities to export primary products. The vent for surplus is indeed a compelling concept, especially in the way it explains the events pertaining to the primary export boom in North America.

During this period when the primary export boom was transforming North America, Continental Europe was rapidly industrializing, gaining ground on England, the first country to industrialize. Industrial exports were pouring forth from France and Germany, invading markets across the globe. In fact, an increase in demand for food from a rapidly industrializing population in Europe is what caused the growth of agricultural exports in North America. The effort and the energy that trade brought forth in North America was matched by similar gusto in Europe. Rewards to human effort were increasing across the continents. In Europe there was no surplus of land, but industry does not require much land. It requires entrepreneurial effort to acquire know-how and transmit it to the labour force. It requires savings to build plants and machines. It requires infrastructure like railroads and ports. The supplies of all these resources can be increased because they are products of human effort. Given appropriate incentives, the surplus of leisure in European society got vented. The vent for surplus process generated gains for primary-exporting North America as it did for industrial-exporting Europe. Trade was indeed an engine of growth for both the trading partners.

But much of the Third World has been a primary-exporting region for the last hundred and fifty years, and it still remains underdeveloped. In the middle of the nineteenth century, India too was a major exporter of wheat, cotton, and indigo to Great Britain. Yet, the Indian economy grew little through the nineteenth century. The forces that propelled economic development in North America seemed to be inoperative in India. In fact, as mentioned earlier, some Indian historians have claimed that the trading relationship with Great Britain may have created poverty in India while it created wealth in Great Britain. Trade was an engine of growth only for Great Britain, but not for her trading partner from whom she imported primary goods. Thus, the trade between India and England had an asymmetrical impact not only on wages but even on the national incomes of the two countries. This is intriguing in the light of what we know about the mutually beneficial nature of trade between Europe and North America. In what respects did India differ from North America that the outcomes of engaging in trade should be so different in the two cases?

A major difference was that in the nineteenth century India had a relatively smaller amount of surplus land of good quality that could be brought under cultivation. In other words, the supply of land could not be expanded as easily as in North America, and any increase in the price of wheat or cotton resulted merely in making the landowners richer without increasing the supply of any inputs in the economy. It can be seen, therefore, that the vent for surplus process was stymied in India since the supply of land could not expand in a country in which most of the cultivable land had already been cultivated. But the argument does not rest there. Recall from the model of trade between India and England in the last chapter that as cheaper Textiles from England poured into Indian markets Indian industry shrank. The industrial workers who lost their livelihood joined the ranks of the agricultural labourers. As the land-to-labour ratio went down in the economy, so did the wages. Although the supply of land remained relatively fixed, the supply of labour could change in response to changed incentives. As the wages went down so did the supply of labour. The logic of the vent for surplus may have worked in the opposite direction in the case of India. Her production may have shrunk as a result of trading with England. The process at work in England, however, was no different from the process evident in Europe in its trade with North America. England's industrial sector was expanding and the wages were increasing. In response to improvement in the rewards to work, the labour supply was increasing. England was getting the full benefit of trade as she was able to vent the surplus of her leisure. The trading relationship was clearly asymmetric in the way the gains were distributed across the two parties.

We saw earlier that trade has two distinct effects. First, trading according to comparative advantage allows an economy to consume at a higher level without any expansion of the overall production capacity. Second, trading can induce greater amounts of productive inputs to be supplied through its effect on the prices of inputs, and thus cause an expansion of the overall production capacity. The process of the vent for surplus as envisioned by Myint assumed that trade would cause the production capacity to expand, and thus, the two effects would reinforce each other. And surely, they did for a primary exporting economy that was not constrained by the amount of natural resource (land, in our example) at its disposal. For India, it was indeed impossible to increase cultivated land at a rate commensurate with the rate at which agriculture had to absorb labour. Under the circumstances, the production capacity of the economy could only shrink. The two effects of trade thus countered each other. Given this, it is not certain at all that, on balance, the effect of trade for India was to increase the total amount of consumption goods available to its population. India's GNP, the total value of its final products, could even have fallen as a result of her trade with England.

Indeed, there are many examples in Asia, Africa, and Latin America of countries that experienced primary export booms without experiencing booms in their national incomes. When the availability of the natural resource that was the source of primary exports was so abundant that more could be brought under production in response to a higher demand, the production capacity expanded and the economy boomed. The economies of Canada and the United States at the turn of the century and those of oil-producing Gulf countries today fall into this category. But these are more the exceptions than the rule. For many other countries the natural resource, whether it is land for an agricultural producer or mineral deposits for a mineral exporter, tends to be more or less fully employed and any attempt to increase production by applying more labour to it is subject to diminishing returns. India, in the long run, may not have much of a future as a primary exporter.

There is, however, something intriguing about our conclusion that a country's national income can possibly decline as a result of engaging in trade. A voluntary exchange, and that is all we are assuming trade is, should not make any party worse off (unless there was something that the party failed to foresee before agreeing to the exchange). To an economist, the answer would be clear. Income is not the sole measure of well-being, he would say. Leisure too is important, and people obviously trade one off against the other. In fact, this is the reason why a fall in wage makes the labour supply decline (as workers choose to consume more leisure). Therefore, it is quite conceivable that in a trade between Singh and Jones, Singh's income declines and yet he is better off as a result of being able to consume more leisure.

Of course, we are ignoring possibilities that involved either coercion of one country by another or simple ignorance that led to erroneous decisions. There have indeed been such examples, in history, of countries being plundered by more powerful countries, or of countries whose leaders misread the available information and made bad decisions. Our purpose at hand, however, is to create a conceptual framework that would allow us to search for the right set of policies. It is reasonable to assume that modern India is free to follow her own will, and that the information available to policy makers is not so limited that all policy making is reduced to taking shots in the dark. Let us, therefore, regard trade as an exercise in voluntary exchange. But if we do, the traditional argument is sound and we should conclude that trade is potentially advantageous to both parties. However, in the context of economic development there is much that the traditional argument ignores. Indeed, an individual can trade income off against leisure and be equally well off. But it may be more desirable for a society anxious to develop that this individual chooses less leisure. Of course, an individual is the best judge of what he should do to maximize his own welfare. The superiority of decentralized decision making, symbolized by the Invisible Hand of Adam Smith, stems from this simple principle. But, this cardinal principle is based on the assumption that the consequences of one's actions are fully borne by oneself. This is a bad assumption to make while thinking about a developing economy. When an individual decides to take a certain action that either confers benefits or imposes costs on others, it is easy to see that his choice of action would not necessarily correspond to what is socially most desirable. The implications of his actions would remain external to the selfish calculations that his decision was based on. In the jargon of economics, such situations are said to be characterized by *externalities*. The process of economic development is replete with externalities of various sorts, as recent academic research recognizes.

Consider, for example, a farmer who decides that it is not worth his while to learn how to read and write. But his ability to read and write may confer benefits on others. Some special knowledge he might possess could find an outlet through his improved communication skills, and diffuse to others. His decision to remain illiterate may thus be rational from his individualistic point of view but sub-optimal from society's viewpoint. In fact, this same farmer might not be averse to becoming literate if he knew that most farmers in his province were becoming literate. There is not much point in learning to write, if the people he is likely to communicate with cannot read. But if they would learn to read, he would not mind making the effort to learn to write. It would be in the interest of the society, therefore, that each farmer spent his time learning to read and write rather than consuming leisure.

For exactly the same reasons, it would be socially more desirable for a worker to attain a given level of well-being through a greater effort rather than through greater leisure. Effort begets effort. Leisure has no externalities. In our simple model, workers represent all those who earn their livelihood by exerting themselves, and landlords represent the rentiers. We have couched the whole discussion in terms of a fall in wages causing a decline in the amount of labour (effort) supplied. But it is even more appropriate to apply the reasoning to entrepreneurial effort (i.e. producer's effort). The entrepreneur is the one who looks for market opportunities to mobilize resources for organizing production. As the price of Textiles, our representative industrial good, falls, it lowers the returns to entrepreneurship, and when entrepreneurs are induced to consume more leisure, an economy stops developing. Labour is often a complement to entrepreneurial effort and so is capital. Whatever induces greater entrepreneurial effort will also induce an increase in the supplies of other augmentable factors like labour and capital.

There are externalities even across efforts of different producers. Suppose a steel manufacturer expends resources to improve productivity and thus lowers the costs in steel production. The lower costs result in lower prices of all the goods that use steel as an input, which increases the purchasing power of everyone in the economy. This, in turn, gets translated into higher demands for the products of other manufacturers, increasing the returns to their efforts and spurring them to increase their productivity. The lowering of the costs of their products due to the resultant productivity growth generates benefits to everyone in the economy. Thus, effort by one producer can create externalities for another producer.

The application of effort by one individual ripples through an economy, inducing greater effort from others and generates for society benefits that the individual had never intended. The other side of this, of course, is that anything that is responsible for discouraging a potential entrepreneur from applying effort would result in a sequence of foregone opportunities and income. Once we take into account these externalities related to effort, it is possible to sustain the argument that a primary export boom caused by an increase in demand resulting from industrial productivity growth abroad could make an economy worse off. The conventional theory which asserts otherwise does not take into account externalities that loom large in the process of economic development.

Coming back to our theme on the pattern of trade, a desirable feature of industrial exports is that they induce effort. Primary exports, on the other hand, may only increase rents to natural resources and, through a decrease in wages, could in fact dampen effort. Tourism could also be thought of as a primary exporting industry. Beautiful beaches and lush green mountains are certainly important natural resources. A picturesque, underdeveloped country would naturally have a comparative advantage in tourism. It could satisfy the demand for industrial products of its population by buying imports with the foreign exchange revenues its tourism generates. What is wrong, one might ask, with not developing an industrial sector at all for such an economy? The answer is simply that, in the long run, the most important resource of all, human effort, would become subject to diminishing returns, because the natural resource here is fixed and the economy would stagnate. A successful development policy must create incentives to increase human effort, and this is one important reason why India should strive to become an industrial exporter. Trade would then work for India as an engine of growth.

The above discussion needs to be qualified, however. Primary exports can also create incentives for farmers to increase their effort. We are assuming that incentive effects are likely to be higher when an entrepreneur's effort is not handicapped by the fixity of complementary resources (like land). It is for this reason that we regard exporting industrial rather than agricultural products as an engine of growth in the long run.

But countries trade according to their comparative advantage.

Most countries are agrarian economies before they industrialize and can hardly be expected to be able to export industrial goods to the rest of the world. In order to develop a comparative advantage in industrial products they must first increase their industrial productivity at a rapid rate. This brings us back to the closing theme of our last chapter. The task of generating rapid industrial progress is exceedingly difficult for some countries but not so for India. How best to carry it out is a crucial question and this is the question we will turn to in our next chapter.

9

Development Policy and Industrial Productivity Growth

We have seen that though industrial productivity increases may not alleviate poverty in a closed economy, they can be very effective in an open economy oriented towards industrial exports. By international standards, the growth in the productivity of Indian industry has been appalling. In this chapter we seek to understand why this has been so. Many of the reasons are to be found in the explicit policies India has implemented with regard to industry. We turn to an examination of the genesis of these policies and of their economic consequences.

It was inevitable that the developmental policy of a country that had just managed to free itself from colonial rule would make self-reliance its main theme. By any measure, the economic performance of the Indian economy under colonial rule had been dismal. India had remained largely a stagnant, agrarian economy exporting primary products to the growing economy of Great Britain. Relying on trade with a developed country had spurred neither industrialization nor growth. It was not surprising, therefore, that trade played a very small role in India's developmental programme in the immediate post-Independence period. Instead, self-reliance was adopted as the main objective.

Self-reliance meant developing the capacity of the economy to be able to produce a wide mix of products so that it would not have to rely on imports. The sectors to be given priority were identified by looking at what the country had been importing, and investment was then undertaken simultaneously in many sectors to substitute for these imports. But in order to produce rayon fabric, for example, the manufacturer would have to import not only the machinery to produce the fabric, but also the material itself, or at least the chemical ingredients from which the material is made. The logic of self-reliance dictates that, if possible, imports of these inputs should also be eliminated. Thus, in order to be able to do without imports alogether in this chain of production, the country would have to develop indigenous chemical, machinery and steel industries. This prescription has been followed in India over the last forty years. As a result, India today has become a diversified economy with the capability of manufacturing sophisticated products like computer and jet planes.

Creating a new industry, however, is an achievement that is qualitatively different from improving productivity in an existing industry. We have seen in the foregoing chapters, that only rapid growth in the productivity of labour can have any real impact on the well-being of the poor. In this chapter, we will discuss why the policies which succeeded in diversifying the Indian economy have failed to bring about rapid productivity growth in industry.

The acceptance of self-reliance as the goal of development has some inevitable policy implications. First, any new industry has to be shielded from international competition for some time. Production costs cannot be lowered without acquiring a detailed knowledge of the productive process, and that takes time and experience. It is as if an industry at its inception is an infant that needs to be protected from competition with the industries that have already reached adulthood in developed countries. Indian industry, though no longer an infant, continues to be heavily protected by various barriers to trade such as tariffs (which make imports more expensive relative to the domestically produced goods) and quotas (which restrict the quantity of imports).

Second, investment has to be guided into sectors deemed appropriate by the government. If it were left to market forces, investment would go into those sectors that offered the highest profits to entrepreneurs. Which sector happens to be the most profitable to a given entrepreneur would depend on the demand for the product he offers. There is no reason to believe that the preferences of consumers are compatible with the government's. This problem was tackled in India by instituting a system of investment licensing. This required an entrepreneur to acquire a government licence prior to undertaking any private investment, and investment was allowed only according to the government's priorities.

Third, it is quite conceivable that there are sectors which rank high on the government's priority list and yet attract no private investment. This could be because there is no market demand for the products of these sectors. This could also happen if there is no entrepreneur with suitable expertise or if the risks associated with the venture are perceived to be too high. In such cases, public enterprises (firms owned and operated by the government) would be needed. In fact, it was reasoned that the viability of sectors like steel, heavy machinery, and chemicals, which produced key inputs for the rest of the economy, should not be left to the vagaries of the market. These sectors, referred to as the *commanding heights* in the Second Five Year Plan, were reserved exclusively for the public sector. Public sector investment in India, however, has not been confined to the commanding heights; even some textile mills and bakeries have been absorbed in the public sector. Today, about 71 per cent of the total employment in the organized sector and 60 per cent of the total industrial capital in India are in the public sector.

A cherished goal of India's development policy, in addition to self-reliance, has been to create a socialistic form of society. Given the status-ridden structure of Indian society and the tremendous gulf between the rich and the poor, the intellectual appeal of socialism in India has been powerful. The industrial licensing system attempted to transfer decision-making from the market, which catered to consumers with money, to government bureaucrats, who take their orders from people's freely elected representatives. The licensing system thus seemed to enhance the power of the poor at the expense of that of the rich. Also, to the extent that what often separates the rich from the poor is the ownership of land or capital or some other asset, an increase in public ownership of productive assets has always been advocated as the classical solution to the problem of inequality. Thus, both the implementation of the industrial licensing system and the dominant presence of public enterprises were compatible with socialist ideals.

Let us now examine how the growth of industrial productivity in India has been affected by each of the three main instruments of India's industrial policy, namely protective trade barriers, industrial licensing, and the dominant role of public enterprises.

Protective Trade Barriers and Industrial Productivity Growth

The purpose of any protective trade barrier is to make it difficult for imports to compete with domestically produced goods. No protection would be needed if the domestically produced goods were cheaper or of better quality than the imports. It is easy to see that if a good being protected were an input required to produce another good, the policy of protection would be directly responsible for raising the production costs of the latter good. For example, protecting the steel industry would inevitably raise the prices of kitchenware made from stainless steel. Clearly, a manufacturer of pots and pans would be working with a handicap if he aspired to export his products while he was buying high-priced steel from a domestic steel producer.

However, we are interested in knowing not only whether production costs would be higher with protection than without, but also whether barriers created to impede imports, in fact, impede the growth of productivity at home. If the only problem with protection was that it made inputs more expensive to prospective exporters, it could be solved simply by remitting the import duties (tariff collected on the inputs) back to them. This would be equivalent to making the required inputs available to them at international prices, thus removing any disadvantage created by the protective policy. In fact, such a policy is already in effect today in India.

The most significant consequence of protecting domestic industry is that the absence of international competition may mean the absence of competition altogether. The lack of competition, in turn, may hamper productivity growth. Since none of these two propositions is self-evident, let us examine them.

First, why would there not be any domestic competition in the absence of international competition? A developing country invariably has at best a small group of people rich enough to have a significant demand for industrial goods. This is true even of a large country like India. The country may be populous, and its large population may be desirous of consuming industrial goods but without purchasing power their desires cannot get translated into market demands. Yet, modern industrial technologies, in contrast to cottage industry technologies, tend to be such that they cannot be operated on a very small scale. Machines, factories, etc. cannot be made arbitrarily small; they have to be larger than some minimum size. If the volume of output is small, however, the costs of machinery, of renting the factory space, and of the overheads get spread over that small volume, giving rise to high costs per unit of the product. For example, consider a plant for producing automobiles. Suppose it costs a minimum of Rs 10 million to build the plant, and to produce each car costs an additional amount of Rs 30,000 (for material, labour, etc.). Now if the firm produced only 100 cars, the cost per car, on average, is Rs 130,000. If the output is increased to 1,000 cars, the cost per car, on average, is only Rs 40,000. In other words, the larger the output the lower is the average cost of producing each car. To produce a small volume of output is thus inefficient (i.e. the average cost is high). But if the market demand is small, firms may have no option but to produce on a small scale. Many industries in India are plagued by the inefficiency stemming from the smallness of markets.

An important implication of the smallness of an industrial market is that only a few firms will suffice to satisfy the consumers' demand. This, too, is characteristic of many industries in India. A consequence of this is that these industries are not competitive. We have seen that in a perfectly competitive market, each firm perceives itself to be such a small part of the market that it has no freedom to raise the price it charges. While all firms would prefer higher prices, any firm that attempts to raise its price would lose all its customers to its rivals. If the technology permits a lower price then the price will be lowered because individual firms, in the hope of capturing the entire market, will cut prices. But when there are only a few firms in an industry, it is possible for them to get together and for all to simultaneously raise prices; they can increase their profits at the expense of consumers. An extreme case of this occurs when the industry is a monopoly, i.e. has only one firm. Thus, while competitive markets have the virtue of forcing the price to as low a level as the prevalent technology would permit, this is not true of industries with only a few firms.

If we want to think about growth in industrial productivity, however, we can no longer take the technology as given. We have to carry our line of reasoning further and ask if there are any grounds to believe that competitive markets would lead to more rapid technical progress and hence to a faster decline in production costs. There are no compelling answers in the academic literature on this issue, but we will present some arguments that seem plausible in the context of Indian development.

Consider a firm that has secured the privilege of being the only firm (a monopolist) to produce steel. It will be able to charge a higher price to its customers and earn higher profits than it could in the presence of competitors. Even if it makes little effort to innovate and cut costs, its monopoly position may allow it to reap substantial profits. If another firm enters the industry, innovates and succeeds in reducing costs, it will be able to capture the market by cutting prices. Exposure to competition creates the threat of extinction and with it the loss of lucrative monopoly profits. This insecurity itself can work as a compelling force to persuade a firm to continually look for ways and means to lower its own costs. A competitive pressure felt by firms serves a very useful social function by ensuring that nobody stops innovating.

But, of course, there is no reason to believe that a monopolist would not try to innovate and cut costs. Since lower costs imply higher profits it would be rational even for a monopolist to innovate. The extent to which resources will be devoted to innovation, however, is determined by their opportunity costs in alternative uses, and these in turn are determined by the environment that pervades the economy. We argue below that the environment pervading the Indian economy discourages innovation since that is a relatively *more expensive* way for producers to increase their profits. Skilled manpower, it turns out, finds its most profitable use in doing jobs such as shuffling paper, securing government licences, cultivating government officials, etc., which are wasteful from society's point of view. The absence of competition allows the firms to remain profitable despite their neglect of innovation. The insulation of domestic firms from foreign competition thus contributes to the problem of low

productivity growth by allowing the socially undesirable allocation of resources to continue.

Let us illustrate the above argument by an example which,
though fictitious, portrays the plight of many entrepreneurs in
India. Consider an innovative electrical engineer who designs a
medical instrument that has a market in the US. If he can deliver
a prototype within a year he is assured of a lucrative order, but if
he cannot, the prospective buyer will look elsewhere. While most
of the necessary circuit components can be purchased in India, a
sophisticated oscilloscope he needs for testing his prototype is
available only from Tektronics, an American firm. So he applies
for an import licence. When three months pass without any ac-
knowledgement, he flies to New Delhi to enquire. He is just one
of many such people visiting the office of the licensing agency
for the same purpose. Finally, when he receives audience with
the official-in-charge he is told that he has to prove that an
equivalent oscilloscope is not made in India. If an Indian firm is
producing such a product it should be protected from foreign
competition, he is told. He is advised to advertise in four major
newspapers published in different cities, specifying the kind of
oscilloscope he needs, and if nobody answers within three
months he would receive permission to import what he wants.
Since this would leave only six months to finish the project, he
has only two options: to abandon the project, or to persuade a
more senior government official to reverse the decision of his
subordinate. Either way, entrepreneurship in this case is reduced
to pushing one's case in the licensing office. Instead of being en-
couraged to spend his time in his laboratory, an innovator is
forced to allocate his time and money in a socially wasteful way.
Ironically, it is a policy designed to protect Indian producers that
is responsible for frustrating the aspirations of this Indian
producer.

There are two distinctly damaging effects of the government
regulation in the above example. First, a substantial chunk of the
entrepreneur's time is absorbed in activities that do not increase
the nation's output. Second, by lowering the returns to an
entrepreneur's effort, it invariably dilutes the entrepreneur's incentives to apply his creative efforts. The country is doubly hurt
by this. Since these unintended consequences of the protection of
domestic producers are very serious for the long-term growth

potential of the country, the virtues of blanket rules of this nature are dubious. The loss of its entrepreneurs' creative skills either through apathy or, possibly through emigration to less stifling environments, is probably the greatest cost to India of the intricate network of government regulations.

Investment Licensing and Industrial Productivity Growth

The investment licensing system in India had several objectives: to guide the industrialization process according to the government's priorities, to maintain a regional and locational balance, and to minimize the possible conflicts between the effects of change and notions of social justice. These are all laudable goals for a developing country, and yet the implementation of the policies formulated to further these goals has impeded the growth of productivity. The main reason for this unintended outcome, again, is that the policies have distorted the incentives facing entrepreneurs and have made innovation more difficult by reducing their freedom to act.

Let us once again use a fictitious, but representative, example to make a point. Consider an entrepreneur working in a paper factory who observes that, despite high tariffs, Imperial Tobacco Company (ITC) imports large amounts of the metal-coated paper used inside cigarette cartons to keep the tobacco moist. If he could produce this paper domestically, he would be contributing to the national goal of self-reliance by substituting for imports. Since ITC would be a captive buyer, no marketing effort would be necessary on his part. As long as he was allowed to import a fully-automated machine, he would require no more than half-a-dozen workers, and thus even training his workforce would be an easy task. Since ITC is currently paying high tariffs on this input, he can charge ITC a high price, ensuring high profits for himself. Yet, once he secures a licence, he has no reason to fear competition from any other firm which might enter the scene on account of the lucrative profits. The licensing agency would never grant another licence to produce a product when the domestic needs were being fully met. As long as the

entrepreneur installs a capacity large enough to satisfy any increases in demand that might arise in the foreseeable future,
entry by another firm can be prevented. But since there must be
others with the same idea, getting the licence becomes the main
challenge. How can he ensure that it is he who gets the licence?
He must find a unique way to woo and influence the appropriate
official in the licensing agency. The quality of being able to secure
a government-ordained privilege is thus the key to becoming a
successful entrepreneur in India. This quality, however, performs
no useful social function. The time and effort expended by the
entrepreneur in securing the licence must be regarded as a social
waste since it bestows no benefits on society; it is irrelevant, from
society's point of view, who gets the licence. If, instead, he had
spent the same time and effort improving productivity, society
would have reaped the benefits of a decline in the price of a
product. In addition, the new idea might have found applica-
tions in other related processes.

In the above example, the source of inefficiency is the government regulation of disallowing entry into an industry when the
domestic needs are being currently met by an existing firm. This
regulation essentially gives the first firm the privilege of being a
monopolist and earning substantial profits. The attraction of
these profits forces an entrepreneur to devote resources to ensure
that it is he who becomes the monopolist. In the absence of
government intervention, the market bestows this privilege on
the firm that can produce the product at the lowest cost, and
hence society benefits. When the government sets up the above
regulation, an unintended consequence is that this privilege is
bestowed on the entrepreneur who is most adept at cultivating
government regulators. The activity of wastefully expending
resources for the purpose of securing this privilege is referred to
as *rent-seeking*.

In a well-functioning capitalist system, an entrepreneur is the
agent of change. He looks for opportunities to improve upon the
status quo, to cut costs, to conceive of better products, etc. He is
motivated by the prospective rewards to him for his efforts, but
society benefits through an improved productivity and cheaper
products. He invents new ways of doing things that render the
old ways obsolete, and new products to replace old products. A
new firm enters a market with a new technology to lower costs.

If successful, it cuts prices and captures the market; if not, it exits. There are myriad experiments, a few of which succeed and the rest fail. Productivity growth occurs when new ideas make room for themselves by pushing aside old ones. As more productive firms enter, less productive firms are destroyed because they cannot compete. Schumpeter, the famous Austrian economist, described this march of productivity growth as *the process of creative destruction*. It is the essence of the dynamism of the capitalist system which, despite all its inherent contradictions, finds a way to rejuvenate itself and to adapt itself to a changed environment.

Clearly, if we take away the freedom of entrepreneurs to profit from opportunities when they present themselves or hinder the entry of more productive firms, or prevent the exit of less productive firms, we would be blocking the process of natural selection of ideas. Bad ideas will then persist, old technologies will remain in place and the growth of productivity will be stifled. It is easy to see what kind of entrepreneur will flourish in such an environment. He will not be the risk-taking problem solver, nor will he be the creator of new ideas and products. He will be the politically astute individual, who knows how to befriend officials and manipulate the government machinery. The greatest drawback of India's regulatory regime has been that it has inadvertently raised the returns to the socially wasteful activity of political manipulation. Consequently, even the innovators are left with no choice but to spend their time winning government approvals for their projects. In fact, the less adept they are at this, the greater is the amount of time they must spend on it.

The political process working through lobbies and pressure groups can also be an impediment to the process of creative destruction. For example, suppose Tatas finds that one of its old textile mills in Maharashtra is unprofitable and should be closed down. By stopping the drain on its profits, Tatas could increase its investment in other more profitable businesses in another area. Suppose, for example, Tatas could open a new chemical plant in Tamilnadu if it is allowed to close the old textile mill in Maharashtra. The closure of the old facility would mean a loss of employment for 1,000 people. These people would, in all likelihood, form a pressure group, make a representation to the government, and try to prevent the closure. The members of this group are well identified. They already have a union to represent them. Their loss is real, and a political party would be willing to take up their cause. But Tatas' decision would generate potential winners along with losers. The new facility would create employment for 1,000 unemployed workers. If these workers could all organize, they would form a pressure group to dissuade the government from hindering Tatas' plans. But clearly, it is not known which 1,000 workers will get these jobs. The workers are faceless at the time the decision is being contemplated. There is no question of any organization being formed. Besides, the gains are hypothetical and hence no political party would be willing to take up their cause. The issue is then cast as a conflict between workers and capitalists, and the unemployed workers who would have otherwise found employment are left out of the public discussion.

The dynamism of capitalism works through the process of creative destruction which generates winners as well as losers. By its very nature, the political process in India is conducive to the formation of pressure groups that would defend the potential losers. The potential winners remain under-represented. This often prevents desirable changes from taking place. The poor, who are mostly outside the organized sector, are the least well-represented group in the society.

What we have described above, however, is only the tip of the iceberg. The course that an Indian entrepreneur must navigate is littered with obstacles. Approval is required to produce a new product at an existing plant. There are products reserved for the small scale sector and the large scale sector is forbidden to produce them even if it could produce them more cheaply. Firms do not have the freedom to shift their investment from one sector to another in order to retrench labour. Some goods like steel, cement, fertilizers, sugar, paper and drugs have been under a regime of administered prices which are typically calculated on a cost-plus basis, i.e. firms receive a price in excess of all of their costs, no matter how exorbitant. Clearly, there is little incentive to undertake any effort to reduce costs under such a system. The regulatory regime in India, of which the industrial licensing system is only a part, has thus reduced the effectiveness of India's entrepreneurs in performing their natural role as innovators.

Public Enterprises and Industrial Productivity Growth

Another key feature of Indian development policy has been the prominent role assigned by it to public enterprises. In addition to reserving the infrastructural industries such as railways, telecommunications, air transport and defence, public enterprises were given preference for licences in other basic industries like steel, capital goods (machine tools, heavy electrical equipment, etc.), and oil refineries. Over time, due to the reluctance of the government to allow firms to fail, unsuccessful firms from different sectors have been picked up by the public sector. These firms have been kept in operation by means of subsidies financed by the general revenues obtained by taxing the public at large. The National Textiles Corporation, for example, harbours many such textile mills that failed in the private sector.

There are two main avenues through which the performance of public enterprises affects the growth of industrial productivity in India. First, since 20 per cent of the total output in the manufacturing sector is produced in the public sector, productivity growth in the public sector has a direct bearing on the overall productivity growth in the economy. Second, since the public sector produces inputs (especially services like transportation, communication, and banking) that are crucial to almost every sector of the economy, its inefficiencies naturally affect the competitiveness of the users of these inputs, as well as their incentives to innovate.

We have tried to argue throughout this chapter that the dismal performance of the Indian private sector in improving productivity could be attributed to two undesirable consequences of the regulatory regime: entrepreneurs have little freedom to respond in a timely fashion to market opportunities, and their incentives are so distorted that they are better off spending their resources in socially wasteful activities. Both these reasons for low productivity growth apply even more strongly to the public sector. The manager of a public enterprise has little autonomy in decision-making. A public enterprise is a convenient patronage device in the hands of the politicians, used to reciprocate favours they have received. Even the location of a new plant is often decided on the basis of short-run political gain rather than on the basis of cost–benefit analysis. If the opposition seems to be gathering strength in Gujarat, the government may shift the refinery originally planned for Madhya Pradesh to Gujarat, even if Madhya Pradesh is the more rational choice on the basis of economics. If Thakur Mansingh delivers twenty parliamentary seats to the ruling party, the favour is returned by placing a telephone factory in his region, whether or not this is warranted on economic grounds. Any decision by the manager to change the status quo by changing the technology, the supplier or the product mix could bring on intervention at the ministerial level. The prices, the technology, the size of the labour force, and the destination of the output ought to be the legitimate areas of decision-making for the manager of any enterprise, but they seldom are in an Indian public enterprise.

There are no incentives under such a system for any enterprise manager, however talented, to take measures to improve productivity. Any such measure would mean a change in the status quo. It would mean that there are some losers. Perhaps, some workers have to be laid off. And, even then, success is never guaranteed. There may be few rewards, if any, if he succeeds, but there will be certain punishment if he fails. Besides, there is no punishment for not innovating. There are very few public enterprises in India, in sectors other than oil and gas, that could survive competition, but neither the managers nor the workers in these loss-making enterprises have to suffer any consequences for this state. The government's long hand can reach into the public treasury to support its employees. If there is no punishment for making losses year after year, how can there be any for a failure to innovate? It is easy to see that there are no incentives for a public sector manager in India to innovate.

The inefficiency and the lack of innovation in India's public sector has resulted in high prices (or bad quality) of essential inputs that feed into the rest of the economy, raising its costs. The price of steel in India is several times higher than the international price. It is easy to see what this implies for so many industries that use steel as an input.

Consider, for example, a machine-tool manufacturer who buys inputs like steel, power, and other services supplied by the public sector such as transportation and telephones for Rs 80 per machine tool. He then uses his own labour and capital to process these inputs for which he incurs a cost of Rs 10 per machine tool, and then sells the output for Rs 100 each. Thus, he makes a profit of Rs 10 on each unit of output he sells. Now suppose that the maximum number of machine tools he can sell domestically at any price is 100 per week. When he contemplates a decision to innovate, he weighs the cost of innovation (say, teaching a new technique to his workers) against the extra profits he stands to make by reducing his costs. Suppose the cost of innovation, which is incurred as a lump sum, amounts to Rs 200 when computed on a weekly basis. If he manages to cut his costs by Rs 1 per unit, he will make an extra profit of Rs 100 per week, not counting the cost of innovation. Clearly, he will not find it worthwhile to innovate. The problem is that he cannot reap sufficient returns on his innovation because he cannot sell a large enough volume at home. If he could sell on the international market, he could sell a much larger volume (say, 500 units) and then he would certainly choose to innovate. But the problem is that the price on the international market may be as low as Rs 80. No matter how hard he tries, he cannot compete internationally because his input costs are too high. Some of these inputs are services like power and telephones, which cannot be imported; he has no choice but to use them. If only the public sector had been more efficient and his total input costs were not more than Rs 70, he would have had a tremendous incentive to innovate. Thus, inefficiency in the public sector adversely affects the incentives to innovate across the economy.

To sum up, industrial productivity growth, by its very nature, is the result of entrepreneurial activity. It is an entrepreneur's ability to remove bottlenecks, to create markets where none existed, to think of substitutes when an input becomes too scarce, to conceive of better products and cheaper processes, to experiment and try out new ideas that generate new possibilities. Many of the industrial policies that India has pursued since Independence have stifled entrepreneurial incentives to innovate. This is a compelling explanation for the slow industrial productivity growth in India.

10

Conclusions

In this book, we have tried to address the question: why have the poor in India stayed poor despite four decades of developmental effort? In order to be able to think about this question systematically, we have presented a conceptual framework which we feel is helpful in understanding the essence of the process of economic development. Different chapters stressed different aspects of our answer, and now the time has come to tie them together.

In India, as in the rest of the world, the poor are those who have nothing else to sell but their labour. But even among workers there are differences. Less than ten per cent of India's labour force works for the organized sector where, through collective bargaining, they have managed to raise their wages much above what they could earn elsewhere. The white and blue collar workers employed in large manufacturing and service establishments such as Siemens (multinationals), Tatas (domestic private corporations), railways and banks (service industries in the public sector), Bharat Heavy Electricals (public enterprises) fall into this category. It is possible for them to get high wages because their employers do not operate in competitive markets and so are able to pass on the higher wage costs to the consumers by charging higher prices. These workers are hardly poor. By the poor we mean the workers competing in the labour markets of agriculture and in the informal service sectors (e.g. hawkers, street vendors) throughout India. Their wages are determined by the marginal product of labour in agriculture. Any change in this marginal product affects the well-being of the poor. But the marginal product of labour depends on the efficiency of the technology and on the land-to-labour ratio. Any change that would move labour from agriculture to other sectors would increase the land-to-labour ratio in agriculture and thus improve the well-being of the poor. All the situations that we have analysed, except for a technical change in agriculture, impinge upon the well-being of the poor through their impact on the land-to-labour ratio. It is important to understand the role played by this ratio in our whole analysis.

Another important aspect of our analysis is the structure of demand. The poor spend most of their incomes on food. The rich, on the other hand, do not increase their expenditure on food by very much as their incomes rise. This difference in consumer behaviour across income classes makes the distribution of income a crucial determinant of the composition of demand for various goods. Not only does the income distribution matter for the results of the analysis, but it also matters how poor the poor are. For example, our result that industrial progress in a closed economy confers minimal benefits on the poor follows from the assumption that the poor are too poor to consume any industrial goods. If, through radical land reform, it were possible to lift their living standards by enough so that they become consumers of industrial goods, industrial progress will be beneficial to the poor. The reader should note the links between the distribution of income and the composition of consumer demand. We present below a systematic review of the main results presented in this book.

If there is neutral or labour-using technical progress in agricultural production, wages rise due to two reasons. Not only would there be an increase in the marginal product of labour for a given allocation of labour between the two sectors, but labour will shift from agriculture into industry, increasing the land-to-labour ratio. A sustained increase in productivity in agriculture is thus a potent instrument for improving the well-being of the poor; it not only helps to increase the market wage but it also reduces the price of food. It also helps to expand the size of the industrial sector because, as food becomes cheaper, more money will become available in the budgets of the rich for spending on industrial goods. Technical progress in agriculture is thus the key to industrialization. The primary reason that even the land-abundant countries of North America and Australia have most of their labour force engaged in industrial production is that they managed to bring about tremendous productivity growth in their agricultural sectors. To a significant extent, India's failure to reduce the amount of labour engaged in agriculture has to be attributed to her failure in bringing about more rapid technical progress in agriculture.

The two most important policy instruments available to induce productivity growth in agriculture are irrigation and primary education. In both these areas the performance of the state and the central governments in India has fallen short. Only 60 per cent of the cultivable land that could be irrigated has been irrigated over the last forty years. Without adequate water control, the productivity of fertilizers and high yielding varieties of seeds is limited. The yields of rice, oilseeds, and coarse grains are still much below potential. We should reiterate that we are using irrigation as a proxy for different kinds of public sector investment that would increase the productivity of agriculture. These would include land reshaping, moisture retention measures, soil conservation measures, and extension services.

In the area of education, the performance has been even more disappointing. About half of India's population is illiterate. Few countries in Latin America or Asia have expended less effort on eradicating illiteracy. At the time of independence, there were a number of countries with rates of illiteracy that were comparable to India's. But, whether in communist China or capitalist South Korea, a frontal assault was launched on illiteracy with impressive results within a single generation. If we compare the percentage of total national income spent on education in India with that in any country at a similar stage of development, it is apparent why India has done so badly on the literacy front. Clearly, education has been given very low priority by Indian policymakers. In 1986, the central government expenditure on education was only 2.1 per cent of its total expenditure, while that on defence was 18.4 per cent. South Korea, a nation perpetually in a state of readiness for war with its neighbour to the north, spent 18.1 per cent on education and 29.2 per cent on defence. (The central government expenditure as a percentage of GNP is slightly higher in the case of South Korea than it is for India.) Even within the budget on education, the lion's share has gone to secondary and post-secondary education. The vast majority of India's farmers and farm workers continue to be illiterate. This hampers the diffusion of know-how and limits the possiblities for productivity growth in agriculture.

It is important here to point out that the agrarian structure in India today is based on family-farms and is markedly different from the landlordism (zamindari) of the colonial days. The Indian farmer today is not merely a landlord; he is also an entrepreneur. Incentives for eliciting his effort in improving productivity are of crucial importance in determining the agricultural productivity in India. With this in mind, the above discussion should be appropriately qualified. We have emphasized the role of public investment in agriculture but private investment by farmers also plays an important role in improving agricultural productivity. Restrictions on farmers' freedom of choice can hamper productivity growth in agriculture.

India's main accomplishment since independence has been to produce a diversified economy with a sizeable industrial sector, at least in terms of the output it produces. This, however, has not contributed significantly to reducing the amount of labour engaged in agriculture. In fact, due to population growth, the amount of labour that agriculture has had to absorb has risen over the last forty years. The poor have thus not shared the benefits of industrialization.

Another question that we have tried to answer is: What is it about India's industrialization strategy that has rendered it ineffective in alleviating poverty? The principal goal of India's industrialization strategy has been self-reliance. Imports and exports have constituted a relatively small part of the Indian economy. As a result, the industrial sector in India has geared its production mainly to meet domestic demand. But in a country as poor as India, the demand for industrial goods largely comes from the small segment of the population that is rich; the poor spend most of their income on food. Any growth in industrial productivity makes industrial goods cheaper for the rich consumers without causing any labour to move from agriculture to industry. The land-to-labour ratio and hence wages remain unaffected by industrial progress.

At this point, we would like to reiterate the importance of actions which redistribute wealth, such as land reform. The irrelevance of industrial progress to the poor stems from the fact that the poor do not consume industrial goods. In some inherently wealthy economies characterized by extreme inequality, it is possible that a radical redistribution of wealth would lift the poor to a sufficiently high level of income so that they can afford to consume industrial goods. Industrial progress will then benefit the poor by making one of their consumption items cheaper. In India, this is unlikely even in the event of the most radical land reform, because the population is very large relative to the amount of cultivable land. But any measure that increases the incomes of the poor brings closer the day when the gains from industrial progress will start accruing to the poor also.

India's industrial productivity growth has never been very impressive, but even if it was, the poor would not benefit from it as long as the economy was closed to international trade. This brings to the fore the importance of international trade. If Indian industry can export its products to the rest of the world in exchange for agricultural goods, labour could shift from agriculture to industry in India, raising the wage. International trade thus makes it possible for industrial progress to benefit the poor in a very poor country. Notice, however, that here industrial progress is the cause and trade is a catalyst in the above process. If the Indian economy is opened up suddenly to industrial imports from developed countries, without first ensuring that the productivity growth in Indian industry was sufficiently rapid, the result may be a de-industrialization of India. This would indeed be disastrous for the poor. Trade will improve the well-being of the poor only if there is a simultaneous increase in the rate of industrial productivity growth.

The feeling among intellectuals that a trading relationship with developed countries would be detrimental to the interests of the poor in India has, at its source, the experience of trade during the colonial rule. The pattern of trade then was the reverse of what we have indicated above. Rapid industrial growth in Great Britain created a growing demand for agricultural goods from India. This resulted in a shift of labour from industry to agriculture, thus reducing the wage rate. The poor in India became worse off as a result of its trading relationship with Great Britain.

Trade with the developed world, thus, can either help the poor in India or hurt them, depending upon whose industrial productivity is increasing at a faster rate. Late industrializing countries have one advantage *vis-à-vis* the developed countries. It is easier to adopt an old technology than to invent a new one. The learning and assimilation of know-how invented in the West can occur at a much faster rate than the generation of new inventions. This is what the Southeast Asian economies have accomplished so well during the last thirty years. If India can achieve such fast growth in her industrial sectors, it could become a major industrial exporting nation. If she cannot, India's poor would not benefit from her industrial progress. Certainly, the task will be much harder for India than it was for South Korea or Taiwan, but with her pool of technical manpower and well-developed financial markets it is well within India's reach.

There is yet another avenue through which trade can be beneficial to a developing country which is able to bring about a rapid growth in her industrial productivity. It allows an increase in the rewards for human effort. How much effort people expend does depend upon the reward or compensation they receive for it. An economy in which there are no rewards for creative effort will be a stagnant economy. A new opportunity to export an industrial good could create incentives to put in greater effort. One individual's decision to increase effort can increase the rewards to the effort of another, and can thus induce the latter to increase his effort level as well. The net result is an overall expansion in the productive capacity of the economy. Trade can thus serve as an engine of growth for the whole economy.

What we have established so far is that trade will benefit the poor as long as there is rapid growth in India's industrial productivity. This, however, has not happened, largely because of the regulatory regime that is stifling Indian industry. The policies that have been so successful in diversifying the economy have failed to generate rapid productivity growth on a sustained basis. Diversifying the economy amounts to introducing new productive activities. This is not difficult in a country like India, with its pool of educated manpower among its elite. Entry into an industry guarantees monopoly profits for a prolonged period because the licensing system which sanctioned the first licence is also likely to discourage competition by not granting licences to other firms. This system is similar to a feudal order conferring a right to collect taxes. There will always be people willing to accept such a privilege. It is immeasurably more difficult to generate productivity growth on a sustained basis. The system must create a continuous pressure to improve productivity. The regulatory system in India has abolished the competitive threat of extinction faced by firms which fail to innovate. Moreover, it has created incentives for entrepreneurs and managers to spend their time wastefully in rent-seeking activities. The system has created rents at the expense of rewards to effort, and with undesirable consequences.

Slow productivity growth, however, is not the only undesirable consequence of the regulatory regime. The regulatory power invested in the bureaucracy has had a pervasive impact on the aspirations of the Indian youth. Associated with this power are the rents which have made these bureaucratic jobs into prizes to be sought after. Having access to these government jobs has recently become a major political issue. The fury unleashed in response to the government's announcement that it would implement the Mandal Commission report (recommending an increase in the share of government jobs reserved for backward castes) can hardly be understood without grasping these essential facts about the Indian economy.

Even more important than the power to regulate is the power to allocate resources. Through the system of administered prices and various subsidy schemes the central government can bolster the incomes of some groups in the society at the expense of the rest. The willingness of the politicians to use this power has created incentives for different groups to form lobbies and compete for resources in the political arena. As long as the resources are scarce, there will be competition for them. In a system dominated by the government, the arena is political rather than the marketplace. The difference is that competition in the political arena is less likely to induce productivity growth. For example, the farmer's lobby in India has lobbied successfully for price supports, fertilizer subsidies, power subsidies and concessional government credit. Altogether, this amounts to a sizable part of the government budget. If it were reallocated to irrigation, primary education, the production of fertilizer and power, there would be an increase in the productivity of Indian agriculture.

A perennial problem for economists is their inability to analyse the political arena with the same level of rigour as they do the economic arena. Typically, economists analyse the economic problems under consideration and suggest policy changes under the assumption that the government responsible for the implementation of policies resembles a benevolent dictator. This is a highly unrealistic assumption in the context of any country. The behaviour of the government is itself subject to various political forces. There are power blocks and lobbies trying to influence government policies in order to further their own selfish ends. There is also a clash of ideologies yielding uncertain outcomes. In order to be able to offer a completely satisfactory answer to the question why poverty in India persists, we have to be able to theorize about the origin and the implementation of policies responsible for the persistence of poverty. Unfortunately, we do not understand these political processes deeply enough to offer any enlightening analysis. We have, therefore, confined our analysis to the economic arena, and even there, we have focused on some broad lessons from the process of development rather than on a detailed policy analysis.

These broad lessons, nevertheless, are interesting and important. The key to reducing poverty is moving labour out of agriculture into other productive activities which are not characterized by diminishing returns. An effective way of doing this is by facilitating rapid technical progress in agriculture. Interestingly, technical progress in industry can achieve this result only if the economy is open to international trade and if India can become an industrial exporter. Trade works as a catalyst in the process of poverty alleviation provided there is rapid productivity growth in domestic industry. Neither the nationalistic policies of closing the economy to trade nor the meek acceptance of the prospect of becoming a raw material exporter to the developed world forever are in the interests of the poor. The right-wing advocacy of a drastic liberalization of the regulatory regime and of growth led by exports has theoretical justification even from the point of view of the poor. And so does the left-wing advocacy of land reform and greater public investment in rural projects like primary education and irrigation. The analysis carried out in this book explains why it is good to increase rewards to human effort—a right-wing theme. It also explains why it is bad to increase rents—a left-wing theme. The discussion on the effect of bureaucratic controls on industry and on the importance of the type of good being exported explains why there really is no inherent contradiction between these themes stressed by the two opposing ideologies. An insufficient understanding of these lessons has been at least partly responsible for the persistence of poverty in India.

Index

2720